Welcome!

Whether you're cooking dinner with your family, mixing up drinks with your friends, or seeking culinary inspiration, you'll find what you're looking for in this debut cookbook from Beth and Lexi, the mother-daughter duo behind the popular cooking platform Crowded Kitchen.

In this book, they bring you a diverse collection of 100+ family-tested and social media-approved recipes, delivered from their crowded kitchen straight to yours. You'll find photos for every recipe, menus for special occasions, fresh seasonal ingredients, and easy substitutions and adaptations for various dietary preferences. With simple appetizers, hearty dinners, refreshing cocktails, indulgent desserts, and more, this down-to-earth guide will inspire cooks of all skill levels to prepare delicious dishes to share.

Crowded Kitchen

Crowded Kitchen

No-Fuss Drinks, Dinners, Desserts, and More for Every Type of Gathering

LEXI HARRISON & BETH SINCLAIR

Publisher Mike Sanders
Executive Editor Alexander Rigby
Editorial Director Ann Barton
Art & Design Director William Thomas
Designer Joanna Price
Recipe Photographer & Food Stylist Lexi Harrison
Lifestyle Photographer Nathaniel Smith
Recipe Tester Robert Naugle III
Editorial Assistant Resham Anand
Developmental Editor Emily Stephenson
Copy Editor Tiffany Taing
Proofreaders Bianca Bosman, Monica Stone
Indexer Michael Goldstein

First American Edition, 2026
Published in the United States by DK Publishing
1745 Broadway, 20th Floor, New York, NY 10019

The authorized representative in the EEA is Dorling Kindersley Verlag GmbH. Arnulfstr. 124, 80636 Munich, Germany

26 27 28 29 30 10 9 8 7 6 5 4 3 2 1
001-344563-FEB2026

Library of Congress Number: 2025941370
ISBN 978-0-5939-5874-2

DK books are available at special discounts when purchased in bulk for sales promotions, premiums, fundraising, or educational use. For details, contact SpecialSales@dk.com

Printed and bound in China

www.dk.com

This book was made with Forest Stewardship Council™ certified paper – one small step in DK's commitment to a sustainable future.
Learn more at
www.dk.com/uk/information/sustainability

To family—ours and yours.
Eat well, together.

Contents

Introduction

WELCOME TO OUR CROWDED KITCHEN

We're Beth and Lexi, a mother-daughter duo from southeast Michigan. Cooking has always been a family affair in our house. From the time Lexi and her siblings were born, we always prioritized fresh food and family-centered meals.

As the kids got older, they often expressed an interest in learning how to cook, and they always expressed an interest in eating well. Like with most kids, there was a lot of boxed mac and cheese involved, but there were also early forays into homemade risotto, caramel making with Grandpa, and even crème brûlée. (In retrospect, that last one may have just been an excuse for Lexi's older brother, Travis, to use a culinary torch.)

Our family has always done a fair amount of entertaining, from hosting most holidays, to throwing themed parties (sometimes for no reason at all!), to frequent dinner parties with friends. Everyone had a role—even if that just meant dish drying for the youngest (Bryce).

So, yes, our kitchen has always been pretty crowded and often quite messy, but to us, a crowded kitchen is a happy one. It's also a place where we've created some of our most meaningful family memories. After all, what better way is there to connect with loved ones than through good food and drink?

HOW WE STARTED CROWDED KITCHEN

As a mother and daughter, the two of us have always shared a close connection that goes far beyond food. When Lexi was in high school, Beth took on a part-time job as the school's cross-country and track coach. With a family talent for long-distance running, it's something special that we shared for years, and Lexi was determined to continue her running career in college.

It was then that we first had to develop a working relationship that was a bit separate from home life. Beth was still "Mom" at cross country practice, but she was also "coach," and it was important for us to figure out the line between those two roles.

During those years, both of us also took our passion for cooking a step further. We became particularly interested in nutrition, especially as it relates to fueling our long-distance runs. We started experimenting with creating and customizing all sorts of recipes from scratch, including our Berry-Coconut Breakfast Quinoa (page 37) and Homemade "Gatorade" (you can find this on our website).

Lexi headed off to Amherst College in the fall of 2012 and accomplished her goal of running in college while there. Beth continued coaching and learning more about nutrition, cooking, and how food fuels performance.

At a very small school with fewer than 2,000 students, Lexi had to learn to navigate the minimal dining options. During her junior year of college, she decided to start an Instagram account (@superfoodrunner) to document how she was fueling as a college endurance athlete with limited food options.

A few months later, Lexi and her then boyfriend (now husband) Brent decided at the last minute to spend a semester abroad in Berlin. She knew she wouldn't be able to keep up with posting on Instagram, and Beth had just started taking an online course about plant-based cooking and food photography. It was the perfect opportunity to work together, so Beth took over content creation while Lexi was gone for 4 months.

We continued working together when Lexi returned home for the second semester of her senior year. She graduated with a degree in English literature and started a job at a food-media startup in New York that perfectly aligned with her passions. As is common at startups, she ended up taking on several roles, including photography and videography for large social media campaigns.

After a year of working there and continuing to build @superfoodrunner's social media presence on the side, Brent and Lexi made the decision to move back to Michigan so she could work with Beth full time. In 2017, we rebranded to Crowded Kitchen, since Lexi was no longer running competitively and we felt we needed a more appropriate name for our growing business. Since then, we've launched a website, shared hundreds of new recipes, grown our social media following to several million, and worked with countless food and beverage companies to create custom recipes and food photography.

Over the years, our content has shifted slightly from mostly plant-based to sharing a wide range of recipes, but we've always focused on seasonal produce, whole foods, and delicious family meals. Our audience has grown and changed with us, and nothing makes us happier than hearing from readers who felt inspired to try something new with one of our recipes.

As our business grew, we realized it would be most effective to divide our roles. Beth takes charge on all things recipe development (you have her to thank for just about all the recipes in this book), while Lexi specializes in photography, social media content creation, marketing, writing, and editing.

True to our name, our kitchen has gotten even more crowded over the years. Brent joined the team full time in 2020 to manage the business side of things, and Dad (Todd) has taken on the roles of Chief Dishwasher and Opinionated Recipe Taster. Our two labrador retrievers, Cody and Oliver, are constant kitchen companions too. Oliver, a professional counter surfer, has managed to taste several of the recipes in this book and gives two paws of approval. (Cody, thankfully, sticks to floor cleanup.) In May 2025, Lexi welcomed her first child, Cole, the newest addition to our crowded kitchen.

Working together for the past 8 years, and especially on this cookbook, has been an incredibly special and rewarding experience. A mother-daughter bond is irreplaceable, and it means the world to us that we've been able to share so many exciting milestones, both in our business and life outside of work.

WHAT YOU'LL FIND IN THIS BOOK

The recipes in this book are not defined by any specific dietary category, but they do tend to focus on whole foods, seasonal produce, and balance. We're most inspired by fresh ingredients, and you'll see that reflected in every chapter of this book.

One thing you won't see a lot of is red meat. Both of us were mostly vegetarian from about 2016 to 2021 and have since reintroduced poultry, fish, and some red meat to our diets, but we still prefer to eat vegetarian about half the time. We've found that most of our social media audience has similar dietary habits, with an interest in both plant-based and more traditional cooking.

Beth has a dairy allergy, so many of these recipes have been tested with nondairy alternatives, and we always note when substitutions can be made. In general, the vast majority of recipes in this book can be made vegetarian or plant-based with simple swaps like nondairy butter and milk or plant-based meat alternatives.

You'll find recipes here for just about any occasion. There are plenty of appetizers and sides for entertaining, and there are also lots of salads, soups, and dinners for the everyday.

Every member of our family loves a good craft cocktail, so there are plenty of those too. We're here to convince you that it's actually really easy to become your own bartender. (And often much less expensive, as well!)

Above all, we firmly believe in balance and moderation. We love a good salad, and sometimes we just want Dessert Fruit Salad (page 236), but we also sometimes bake Maple, Bourbon, and Pecan Sticky Buns for breakfast (page 44) or eat half a batch of Pecan, Cherry, and White Chocolate Cookies in one sitting (page 221). Maybe with a Tiramisu Martini (page 210) to wash it down.

Many of these recipes are inspired by friends and family, or special experiences we've had together in the kitchen or while traveling. Try Aunt Irena's Palačinky (Czech Crepes, page 38) for your next Sunday brunch or Brent's famous Lemon Pepper Wings (page 66) for the big game.

This book is meant to inspire you to create more special moments with your family and friends through delicious, well-crafted food and drink. Whether it's a holiday meal or an average Monday night, we hope these recipes bring you comfort, fun, and a whole lot of flavor.

From our crowded kitchen to yours,

Lexi and Beth

Ingredients

Here at Crowded Kitchen HQ, we recognize that this cookbook is not going to be your only recipe resource going forward, so we're not going to give you any specifics on how you should or shouldn't stock your kitchen. However, there are a few ingredients that require a bit of explaining, so without further ado . . .

SALT

Salt is the single most important ingredient you'll need to keep stocked in your kitchen, since it's responsible for adding flavor to just about everything. Believe it or not, the type of salt you use can make a huge difference in how your final dish tastes.

In this book, we always use Diamond Crystal kosher salt, unless otherwise noted. Kosher salt dissolves more quickly and is less salty by volume, which allows you to gradually add flavor to a dish without oversalting it. Kosher salt is not the same as fine sea salt or iodized table salt, which is what you'll find in a saltshaker at a standard restaurant. Table salt has much denser crystals and, therefore, will make your food taste much saltier. We do not recommend using it, but if that's what you have, decrease the amount of salt in our recipes by half, and taste from there.

We also like to keep flaky sea salt on hand for sprinkling atop desserts (like chocolate chip cookies or homemade caramels) or to finish dishes like grilled meats, roasted vegetables, or fried eggs.

Everyone has different tastes when it comes to salt, so the best way to season with it is to do so in layers and to taste the dish often. It's also important to note that naturally salty ingredients like miso, soy sauce, capers, anchovies, cheeses, cured meats, and more will affect the overall saltiness of the dish, so be mindful when making adjustments.

Keep in mind that presalting most cuts of meat is the best way to season the meat from within and retain moisture. Depending on the cut of meat, a recipe may call for a few hours or overnight of presalting, so be sure to read through the recipe ahead of time.

OILS

Olive Oils

You should keep two different types of olive oil stocked in your pantry. Good quality extra-virgin olive oil (EVOO) is best used in dressings, for dipping bread, or in very low-heat applications. EVOO is unrefined and cold-pressed, so it's more flavorful and complex tasting. If you're using olive oil for higher-heat applications, like roasting or sautéing, look for a bottle of regular (light) olive oil, not extra virgin. It will be less expensive and typically lighter in both color and flavor.

High-Heat Oils

Our favorite neutral-tasting, high-heat oil is avocado oil, which has a smoke point of 520°F (270°C). It's great for pan frying, roasting, grilling, and even deep frying. Other neutral oils with high smoke points include grapeseed, sunflower, and peanut oils.

Specialty Oils

We like to keep coconut oil on hand for baking and especially for thinning out melted chocolate to make it easier to dip. Sesame oil is also a staple for adding rich, slightly nutty flavor to dishes. For a super flavorful punch of sesame, we like to keep a small bottle of toasted sesame oil on hand.

VINEGAR

In our opinion, every kitchen should have a few different types of vinegar. It's one of the easiest ingredients for adding depth and acid to batches of homemade dressings, dips, marinades, and more, and each has a slightly different flavor profile. We always have a good-quality balsamic vinegar on hand, as well as balsamic glaze, apple cider vinegar, distilled white vinegar for pickling, red and white wine vinegars, and champagne vinegar, which we use more occasionally for recipes like our Peach, Tomato, and Burrata Salad (page 107).

SWEETENERS

There's a proper time and place for different types of sugar, and you'll see several forms of sugar utilized in this book. Sugar is, of course, essential for sweetening baked goods and desserts, but it's also an important ingredient for balancing salty, sour, acidic, or bitter dishes, like vinaigrettes, tomato sauces, marinades, or glazes, and even some soups and stews. Note that we don't stock sugar-free alternatives such as stevia or monk fruit sweetener and haven't tested the recipes with them. We find the sweeteners below get the job done in our kitchen. While sugar-free alternatives can work well in some recipes (especially hot or cold drinks, simple syrups, sauces and dressings, jams, and chocolate), they do not always work as a 1:1 substitute for baking or caramelizing. Additionally, different sugar-free options taste different and have varying levels of sweetness, so you may have to do some experimenting to figure out what works best for you.

Granulated Sugar

The standard stuff will do! If you do a lot of baking, you may also want to have a tub of coarse turbinado sugar on hand for topping scones, pie crusts, etc.

Brown Sugar

Made from regular granulated sugar and molasses, we mostly use light brown sugar for baking. When a recipe calls for brown sugar in this book, pack it lightly into the measuring cup and level with a knife to ensure accurate measurement.

Honey

Good-quality honey is a go-to sweetener in our household, especially when it's locally sourced. Keep in mind that inexpensive honey at the grocery store often contains other ingredients, like high-fructose corn syrup, so check the label to make sure it's pure.

Maple Syrup

Pure maple syrup can add complex, rich sweetness to a variety of recipes. It works particularly well with fall flavors, like apple cider and cinnamon, and can be used for cocktails, baking, and even savory dishes. (Note: Maple syrup is not the same as pancake syrup!)

Agave

We most often use agave syrup in cocktails or when we need a liquid sweetener but don't want the strong flavor of maple syrup or honey.

INGREDIENT SUBSTITUTIONS FOR DIETARY NEEDS

You will find plenty of vegetarian (V), plant-based (PB), and dairy-free (DF) recipes in this book, but many of the nonveg recipes can also be made vegetarian or plant-based with just a few simple swaps.

Meat

When it comes to ingredients like ground chicken, turkey, or beef, we suggest using a ground plant-based alternative, like Impossible Foods. The taste and texture will be the closest to regular meat, and it's an easy 1:1 swap. If you don't like to use plant-based meat alternatives, we often like to substitute with beans or lentils, especially in a salad or soup.

Tofu is also a great option. For a texture more like ground meat, follow the steps in our Sofritas Tofu Tacos recipe (page 126) for perfectly crispy tofu that can be used in a multitude of recipes.

Whole Milk

The best, most consistent substitute we've found for whole milk is full-fat oat milk. It's much creamier than most plant-based milks and has a mild flavor. Just make sure to purchase unsweetened, unflavored oat milk.

Heavy Cream

If you live in the US, there are multiple brands that make fantastic plant-based heavy cream substitutes that even whip up like regular whipped cream. Our favorites are Silk and Country Crock.

Butter

This is the easiest swap to make. For nonbaking recipes, just use your favorite plant-based butter or olive oil instead. For baking, we suggest sticking to plant-based butter. Our favorite option is Country Crock Plant Butter. Miyoko's is also fantastic, if a little pricier.

Eggs

Eggs can be a bit trickier for a direct substitution and often require making a few more adjustments to a recipe, especially if it's a baked good. If you're making a savory breakfast egg recipe, like our Sheet-Pan Frittata (page 34), you can use Just Egg brand, which makes a liquid that cooks up very similar to real eggs. For baking, our favorite substitute is a flax egg, which is 1 tablespoon ground flaxseed mixed with 3 tablespoons water for one "egg." Stir it together and let sit for about 10 minutes at room temperature to thicken before adding to your recipe. This is not always a 1:1 substitution, so try it at your own risk. (For example, it may work well in baked goods like cookies, brownies, cakes, or quick breads but will not work in recipes like homemade ice cream, puddings, and pâtisserie, like macarons). If you're looking for more plant-based baking recipes, we have plenty on our website, which you can visit at crowdedkitchen.com.

Yogurt, Sour Cream, Cream Cheese, and Other Dairy Products

There are hundreds of plant-based dairy substitutes on the market, and they're all made with slightly different ingredients. Our best advice is to just try a few and find what you like! These are some of the easiest ingredients to use as a 1:1 swap in sauces, soups, toppings, and more.

Cheese

Plant-based cheese sometimes does not melt quite as well as regular cheese but still works as a substitute in many recipes. A few brands we've had good success with include Violife, Follow Your Heart, and Daiya.

Gluten-Free

We can't guarantee that every recipe in this book will turn out the exact same with gluten-free flour, but most popular brands work well for just about any application. Our favorite brand is Bob's Red Mill Gluten Free 1-to-1 Baking Flour. We've also marked naturally gluten-free recipes with GF.

Peanut- or Tree Nut–Free

Any recipes that call for peanut butter can be made with any other nut or seed butter, like almond butter, cashew butter, or sunflower seed butter. Any of our recipes that contain tree nuts can be made with either pumpkin seeds (pepitas) or sunflower seeds instead.

Tools and Techniques

KNIVES AND BASIC KNIFE SKILLS

In our opinion, there's no category of kitchen tools more important than quality knives. Dull knives are less effective, less safe, and make prep work more difficult than it needs to be. The good news is that if you're starting from scratch, you don't necessarily need to invest in an entire 20-piece set of expensive knives.

For most purposes, you can get away with a great 8- or 9-inch (20 or 23cm) and 6-inch (15cm) chef's knife. An 8-inch (20cm) is most versatile and our go-to choice for most uses. It's also essential to have one good-quality paring knife for tasks like trimming, coring, peeling, and mincing. Lastly, you'll need at least one serrated knife. We have two sizes: a 10-inch (25cm) for breads and baked goods, and a smaller 6-inch (15cm) utility knife for delicate produce like tomatoes. We also highly recommend investing in one good pair of kitchen shears.

To keep your knives in tip-top shape, sharpen them at home once every 2 months, and take them in to get professionally sharpened once a year.

The key to becoming a more efficient home cook is knowing and mastering basic knife skills and techniques.

GENERAL KNIFE GUIDELINES

Grip

For the best control and balance, the palm of your hand should be choked up on the handle, and your thumb and forefinger should grip the top of the blade. It takes a bit of practice, but this is the most efficient way to hold a knife (versus wrapping your entire hand around the handle).

Keep Fingertips Safe

Your free hand will help guide the knife and keep the food in place, but be sure to keep your fingertips curled inward (like a claw) at all times.

Rocking Motion

Move your knife in a rocking motion from front to back as you chop.

Stable Surface

If your cutting board is slipping around on your countertop, place a flat damp towel underneath it to keep it in place.

ESSENTIAL COOKWARE

This isn't an exhaustive list but rather the items we use most frequently. Some of the other equipment we recommend for a well-stocked kitchen include a handheld citrus juicer, a meat thermometer and candy thermometer, a mandoline, a basting brush, an electric hand mixer, a rolling pin and silicone baking mat, a vegetable peeler, cheesecloth, and several sizes of rimmed sheet pans, cake pans, and baking dishes.

Enameled Cast Iron

Good-quality cast-iron pots and pans will last you a lifetime. They're versatile, high quality, and they distribute and retain heat evenly, making them an excellent choice for many different cooking methods, like searing, braising, deep frying, roasting, and baking.

We always recommend purchasing enameled cast iron, which does not require seasoning or special care like regular cast iron. The enameled surface is very easy to clean and is resistant to rust and corrosion. Our brand of choice is Staub; their products are handcrafted in France, and as an extra bonus, they're absolutely gorgeous and can double as a centerpiece in your kitchen.

If you're not sure where to start, we recommend investing in a 5.5- or 7-quart (5.2 or 6.6L) Dutch oven, which is perfect for soups, stews, bread, deep frying, and more; an 8.5- or 11-inch (22 or 28cm) skillet for sautéing and pan frying, and a wide 12-inch (30cm) braiser with a lid for one-pot meals.

Stainless Steel

Stainless steel has a steep learning curve, and for that reason, we're more likely to use enameled cast iron for most applications. However, we suggest keeping a few stainless steel pots and pans on hand, especially saucepots, one small skillet, and one larger skillet for larger-batch meals.

Nonstick

Nonstick pans are convenient but shouldn't be your only option. We keep two to three good-quality nonstick skillets and saucepans on hand. Stick to silicone or wood utensils when cooking with nonstick pans, since metal utensils will scratch and wear down the coating.

Blender and Food Processor

We use our blender for blending soups, sauces, dressings, frozen cocktails, and more. A good-quality high-speed blender makes all the difference, and we especially suggest looking for one that comes with a tamper to help push down ingredients for a smoother and easier blend.

Many of the recipes in this book utilize a food processor, and that's because it's one of the handiest tools in your kitchen! We use it for everything from making crusts and doughs to sauces like pesto, homemade sorbet, and nut butters. It's also great for quickly chopping ingredients like nuts and vegetables. Make sure to get a food processor with a few slicer attachments. There's no faster or easier way to shred an entire block of cheese in seconds or thinly shave brussels sprouts.

MEASURING CUPS AND SCALE

Measuring Cups

We use the standard American measurements of cups, tablespoons, and teaspoons, so ensure you have a full set of measuring spoons and cups. It's essential to have a set of liquid measuring cups for the most accurate measurement.

When measuring dry ingredients like flour, we suggest spooning the flour into the measuring cup, then leveling it with a knife for the most accurate measurement. Scooping flour straight from the bag can lead to overpacking, so you may end up with more flour than what the recipe calls for.

Scale

We include weight measurements as often as possible so this book can be used by international audiences. Even if you live in the US, consider measuring by weight! It's more accurate, easier, and leaves you with fewer dishes to clean.

Fine-Mesh Sieve

This is a tool you'll see mentioned frequently in this book. In addition to a regular colander or two for draining and rinsing, a fine-mesh sieve is essential for straining seeds and pulp from sauces and jams; removing herbs and spices from simple syrups, alcohol infusions, and broths; rinsing rice and other grains; and even sifting dry ingredients.

COOKING UTENSILS

Silicone Spatulas

They're versatile, easy to clean, and safe to use with any type of cookware without scratching. We suggest purchasing both large and small silicone spatulas for mixing sauces, batters, or stirring ingredients in a pan or pot.

Microplane

This is helpful for zesting fruit, finely grating garlic or ginger, or grating hard cheese to finish a dish.

Whisks

A large whisk is essential, but keep a small whisk on hand, too, for small-batch sauces and more. Consider purchasing a silicone whisk if you have a lot of nonstick cookware.

Food Waste

How to Keep Your Kitchen from Getting *Too* Crowded

About 40 percent of all food purchased in the US doesn't get consumed—the equivalent of buying five grocery carts full of food and leaving two behind at the store. Not only is that a lot of food waste, but it's also a waste of money (and often space in your fridge and pantry). Food waste is the single-largest segment of landfills in the US and is the biggest source of methane gas production in landfills, so it's important to us to utilize the methods below to keep your kitchen, the planet, and your wallet happy.

PLAN YOUR MEALS

Meal planning (and properly accounting for leftovers) is the easiest way to cut down on waste. Keep a spreadsheet (or a list in your phone's notes app) of your favorite go-to recipes or recipes you want to try soon, and sort them by meal type or difficulty so it's always easy to make a plan for the week. Most importantly, be realistic! If you know your week is going to be stressful, make sure to plan for a night or two of ordering out and don't overbuy at the store. It's also important to plan your portion sizes. If you're only cooking for two and you're not a fan of leftovers, consider cutting a standard recipe in half so you don't end up with waste.

STORE LEFTOVERS PROPERLY

Invest in good-quality storage containers. We particularly love using Zwilling Fresh & Save vacuum-seal containers—the vacuum seal keeps food fresh for up to five times longer in both the fridge and freezer. Always take note of storage instructions in a recipe—most dishes only last for 3 to 4 days in the refrigerator, so if you know you won't eat leftovers that quickly, consider freezing them right away instead. Take it an extra step further and label and date your leftovers so you know if they're still safe to consume.

KNOW YOUR REFRIGERATOR

Keep in mind that your fridge has warmer zones (i.e., the top shelf) and cooler zones (i.e., the bottom shelf), so store highly perishable foods accordingly. Overcrowding your fridge or freezer can also lead to improper circulation. A thermometer placed inside your fridge will help you learn if your refrigerator is being properly cooled (it should be 37°F, 3°C) and where your warm zones are.

USE HIGH- AND LOW-HUMIDITY DRAWERS PROPERLY

High-humidity drawers are for most vegetables, herbs, greens, and anything that wilts easily. Low-humidity drawers are for produce that rots easily, such as most fruits and vegetables like mushrooms. Certain fruits (like apples, pears, avocado, mango, stone fruits, and cantaloupe) produce ethylene gas as they ripen, which causes produce around it to ripen as well. Keep these items stored away from produce that's particularly ethylene sensitive, like greens, berries, beans, and carrots.

THE FREEZER IS YOUR FRIEND!

The freezer isn't just for meal leftovers. Freeze leftover citrus juice, tomato paste, minced garlic and ginger, pesto, juices, sauces, broths, and more in ice-cube trays or silicone freezer trays (we love the brand Souper Cubes). You can also chop

fresh herbs, add them to an ice-cube tray, and fill with olive oil—this is especially helpful at the end of the summer when you have a ton of herbs in your garden. Once the ingredients are frozen, transfer them to a freezer-safe container for long-term storage.

LEARN HOW TO USE SCRAPS

Use carrot, beet, or radish greens in soups, sautés, and sauces and dips, like pesto. Save your Parmesan rinds to use in soups or stews to add a rich umami flavor. There is no need to peel cucumbers, carrots, and other veggies—just wash and scrub them well with a vegetable scrubbing brush. If you do peel your veggies, reserve the peels for your homemade vegetable stock or crisp them up to use as a topping for a dish.

KEEP YOUR KITCHEN ORGANIZED

A messy, overstocked fridge makes it harder for you to tell what you do and don't have. We're all guilty of leaving carrots at the bottom of the vegetable drawer until they're limp beyond saving, but the more often you clean out and take visual stock of the ingredients you already have, the less likely you are to accidentally overbuy. After shopping, move older ingredients to the front of the fridge so you're most likely to use those first.

SHOP WITH A LIST

This is an easy one! Write out a physical list or use your notes app to cut down on impulse purchases. If you're using a specialty item and only need a specific amount (like nuts or dried fruit), consider purchasing from the bulk bin in the exact quantity that you need.

COMPOST

If all else fails, toss leftovers in your compost! It's certainly a better option than contributing to landfills. Some food products you should never add to home compost include meat, dairy, bones, oils or fats, whole eggs, and baked goods. If your city or town composts, always check what they accept before adding any leftovers.

Menu Ideas

HOLIDAY COCKTAIL PARTY

- Cranberry-Orange Whiskey Cocktail (page 209)
- Fruit-and-Nut Crackers (page 49), paired with a cheese and/or charcuterie board
- Spinach and Artichoke Puff Pastry Bites (page 62)
- Shaved Brussels Sprout Salad (page 118)
- Harissa-Roasted Carrots with Tahini-Yogurt Sauce (page 175)
- Pumpkin Ricotta Gnocchi (page 180)
- Pomegranate-Cranberry Caramels (page 247)

SUMMER BARBECUE

- Rosé Lemonade (page 193)
- Grilled Flatbread with Pesto Ricotta, Melon, and Prosciutto (page 69)
- Peach, Tomato, and Burrata Salad with Crispy Breadcrumbs (page 107)
- Citrus-Herb Chicken Kebabs (page 131)
- Zucchini Corn Fritters (page 164)
- Four-Berry Slab Pie with Vanilla-Oat Streusel (page 230)

GAME DAY

- Brent's Lemon Pepper Wings (page 66)
- Loaded Potato Wedge Nachos (page 70)
- Cheesy Corn Poblano Dip (page 57)
- Poblano White Bean Chili (page 146)
- Hot Honey Panko Chicken Cutlets (page 145)
- Frozen Bourbon Arnold Palmer (page 201)

DATE NIGHT AT HOME

- Figs in a Blanket (page 58)
- Roasted Chicken Thighs with Pancetta and Red Grapes (page 149)
- Perfect Herb-Roasted Potatoes (page 167)
- Pan-Fried Shredded Brussels Sprouts (page 176)
- Red Velvet Martini (page 214)

BRUNCH AT HOME

- Bunny Mary (page 189)
- Maple, Bourbon, and Pecan Sticky Buns (page 44)
- Sheet-Pan Frittata with Sun-Dried Tomatoes, Spinach, and Feta (page 34)
- Berry, Avocado, and Spinach Salad (page 100)
- Savory Dutch Baby with Caper-Dill Cream Cheese and Smoked Salmon (page 29)

TACO TUESDAY

- Poblano White Bean Chili (page 146)
- Fish Taco Bowls with Creamy Jalapeño-Avocado Sauce (page 128)
- Pineapple and Passion Fruit Rum Punch (page 217)
- Salted Mango Margarita Bars (page 222)

VEGETARIAN DINNER PARTY

- Roasted Beet and Feta Dip (page 53)
- Loaded Greek Salad Hummus (page 54)
- Roasted Radish Salad with Green Goddess Dressing (page 99)
- White Spinach and Mushroom Lasagna (page 156)
- Dessert Fruit Salad (page 236)

Breakfast

STAUB
SABRE

SERVES 2 | **PREP TIME:** 20 MINUTES **COOK TIME:** 20 MINUTES

Savory Dutch Baby

with Caper-Dill Cream Cheese and Smoked Salmon

A Dutch baby (also known as a *German pancake*) is essentially a large pancake-style popover, with crisp, puffy edges and a custardy interior. It's very similar to the British Yorkshire pudding, but in the US, this is typically served as a sweet breakfast treat, often paired with a fruit filling or compote and powdered sugar. This version is topped with a creamy, herb-forward caper and dill cream cheese spread, plus lots of smoked salmon. A Dutch baby relies on steam in a hot oven to puff up (there is no leavening agent). Make sure your ingredients are at room temperature before blending, and preheat your pan in the oven so it's super hot when you pour the batter in!

FOR THE DUTCH BABY

½ cup all-purpose flour
½ cup whole milk, room temperature
2 large eggs, room temperature
1 tbsp granulated sugar
1 tsp lemon zest
1 tsp chopped dill
¼ tsp kosher salt
2 tbsp unsalted butter

FOR THE CAPER-DILL CREAM CHEESE

½ cup whipped cream cheese
3 tbsp plain Greek yogurt
1½ tbsp chopped dill
1 tbsp capers, drained and chopped
½ tsp grated lemon zest
¼ tsp kosher salt
¼ tsp ground black pepper

FOR SERVING

4oz (115g) smoked salmon
1 mini cucumber, shaved into thin ribbons
Pickled red onions,
(optional; see page 251)
Whole capers
Chopped dill
Ground black pepper, to taste

1. Preheat the oven to 425°F (220°C) and place a 9-inch (23cm) cast-iron skillet in the oven as it preheats.
2. To make the pancake, in a blender, combine the flour, milk, eggs, sugar, lemon zest, dill, and salt. Blend until smooth, scraping down the sides as needed to ensure there are no dry lumps. Let the batter sit at room temperature for 10 to 20 minutes while the oven preheats.
3. To make the cream cheese, to a medium bowl, add the cream cheese, Greek yogurt, dill, capers, lemon zest, salt, and pepper and whisk until combined. Set aside.
4. Once the oven is preheated, carefully remove the skillet and add the butter, swirling it around until it has completely melted and the pan is evenly coated.
5. Pour the batter into the skillet, then return to the oven. Bake for 15 to 20 minutes, until the edges are puffy and golden brown. Don't open the oven while cooking, at the risk of deflating the pancake.
6. Once removed from the oven, add dollops of the caper-dill cream cheese while the Dutch baby is still warm. Top with the smoked salmon, cucumber ribbons, and pickled red onions (if using). Garnish with the whole capers, chopped dill, and black pepper to taste. Serve right away!

MAKES 4 | **PREP TIME:** 5 MINUTES **COOK TIME:** 10 MINUTES

Prosciutto, Sun-Dried Tomato, and Egg Croissant Breakfast Sandwich

Paired with a freshly brewed espresso, this croissant breakfast sandwich will almost make you feel like you're at a French café. If prosciutto isn't your thing, this would be equally delicious with a few slices of crispy bacon. The sun-dried-tomato aioli provides a rich, tangy punch that brings everything together. You can really do the eggs however you like: scrambled, over easy, over hard, even poached.

FOR THE SUN-DRIED-TOMATO AIOLI

½ cup mayonnaise
¼ cup finely chopped oil-packed sun-dried tomatoes, drained
1 tbsp freshly squeezed lemon juice
1 garlic clove, grated
¼ tsp kosher salt
Ground black pepper, to taste

FOR ASSEMBLY

4 large eggs
4 croissants, sliced in half lengthwise
4oz (115g) prosciutto
4 handfuls of arugula

1. To make the aioli, in a medium bowl, whisk together the mayonnaise, sun-dried tomatoes, lemon juice, garlic, salt, and pepper until evenly incorporated.
2. Cook the eggs to your preference. We prefer over easy or sunny-side up in this sandwich.
3. To assemble the sandwiches, on the bottom half of each croissant, spread 1 to 2 tablespoons aioli, then follow with an egg, the prosciutto, a handful of arugula, and the top of the croissant. Serve right away.

450
300
150

SERVES 6–8 | PREP TIME: 10 MINUTES COOK TIME: 50 MINUTES

GF

Smoky Sweet Potato and Sausage Sheet-Pan Hash

Lexi: Any time I try to make breakfast hash in a skillet, it proves to be more trouble than it's worth. The potatoes never quite cook through before they're burnt on the exterior, and it's hard to get the timing right. Enter sheet-pan hash! The easiest way to get all your breakfast favorites on one convenient sheet pan. Potatoes, sausage, peppers, onion, and eggs are all tossed in a slightly smoky spice blend. You can add toppings like avocado or guacamole, cheese, salsa, and hot sauce. This is a great way to feed the whole family with minimal clean up.

1½lb (675g) sweet potatoes, unpeeled and diced into ½-inch (1cm) cubes
1 red bell pepper, diced
1 small yellow onion, diced
1 medium poblano pepper, seeds removed and diced
2 tbsp avocado oil
1½ tsp dried oregano
1¼ tsp chili powder
1 tsp kosher salt, plus extra for the eggs
¾ tsp smoked paprika
½ tsp garlic powder
8oz (225g) cooked chicken or pork breakfast sausage, sliced into ½-inch (1cm) rounds
2 tbsp finely chopped cilantro
6–8 large eggs
Ground black pepper, to taste

FOR SERVING

¼ cup crumbled cotija cheese
Diced avocado
Hot sauce (optional)
Chopped cilantro (optional)

1. Preheat the oven to 425°F (220°C).
2. To a large bowl, add the sweet potatoes, bell pepper, onion, poblano pepper, avocado oil, oregano, chili powder, salt, paprika, and garlic powder. Toss well to coat the vegetables.
3. Transfer the vegetables to a rimmed sheet pan and spread into an even layer.
4. Roast for 25 minutes, stirring halfway through. Remove from the oven and mix in the sausage and cilantro. Return to the oven for 10 to 15 minutes, until the sweet potatoes are fork tender.
5. Using a spatula, create 6 to 8 wells in the vegetable mixture, one for each egg, then crack the eggs into the wells. Season each egg with salt and pepper to taste. Return the pan to the oven and cook for about 10 minutes, until the egg whites are set and don't jiggle when the pan is shaken.
6. Sprinkle with cotija cheese, diced avocado, hot sauce (if using), and chopped cilantro (if using) and serve right away.

Make it vegetarian: Leave out the sausage or substitute with your favorite plant-based alternative.

SERVES 12 | **PREP TIME:** 15 MINUTES **COOK TIME:** 45 MINUTES

Sheet-Pan Frittata
with Sun-Dried Tomatoes, Spinach, and Feta

If you're hosting overnight guests and want to make something a little more exciting than scrambled eggs and toast, this sheet-pan frittata is the way to go. It's easy to throw together, and you can really customize it with just about any vegetables, cheeses, and proteins. Our favorite version has a Mediterranean flair, with sun-dried tomatoes, spinach, feta, and olives. It's hearty, filling, quick, and most importantly, delicious. Aside from hosting, this is a meal prep favorite. Slice and freeze frittata squares for later—they're especially delicious sandwiched between an English muffin or bagel.

- Butter or olive oil, for greasing
- 8oz (225g) bacon, diced
- 8oz (225g) button mushrooms, thinly sliced
- 1 small yellow onion, diced
- 1 cup diced red bell pepper
- ¼ cup pitted kalamata olives, drained and chopped
- 2 tbsp finely chopped oil-packed sun-dried tomatoes
- 1 tsp dried oregano
- ½ tsp kosher salt
- ½ tsp ground black pepper
- 3oz (85g) baby spinach, chopped
- ¼ cup finely chopped parsley
- 18 large eggs
- ¾ cup whole milk
- 1¼ cup crumbled feta cheese, divided

1. Preheat the oven to 375°F (190°C) and lightly grease a rimmed, nonstick 13 x 18-inch (33 x 46cm) sheet pan with butter or olive oil.
2. In a large skillet over medium heat, cook the bacon, stirring occasionally, for about 5 minutes, until the bacon is crispy and the fat has rendered. Using a slotted spoon, transfer the bacon to a plate lined with paper towels, leaving the rendered fat behind. Set aside.
3. To the same skillet, add the mushrooms and onion and cook, stirring occasionally, for about 5 minutes, until the mushrooms are softened.
4. Stir in the bell pepper, olives, sun-dried tomatoes, oregano, salt, and pepper and cook for 3 to 4 minutes, stirring frequently, until the peppers are slightly softened and most of the moisture from the mushrooms has evaporated.
5. Stir in the spinach and parsley and cook for about 1 minute, until the spinach is wilted. Remove from the heat. Add the cooked bacon back to the pan and stir to combine.
6. In a large bowl, whisk together the eggs and milk until no streaks remain.
7. Transfer the cooked vegetable mixture to the prepared sheet pan and spread into an even layer. Sprinkle 1 cup of the feta cheese over the vegetables, then pour the egg mixture over the cheese. Using a spatula, gently stir the eggs and the vegetable mixture. Sprinkle the remaining ¼ cup feta cheese over top.
8. Bake for 25 minutes, until the eggs are set and the frittata is lightly browned around the edges. Let cool for 10 minutes before slicing into 12 rectangles.

Storage instructions: Store in the refrigerator in an airtight container, separated by layers of parchment paper. You can also flash-freeze the squares, then transfer to a freezer-safe container and keep in the freezer for up to 3 months. Defrost overnight in the refrigerator before reheating.

Make it vegetarian: Leave out the bacon or use a plant-based alternative.

SERVES 4 | **PREP TIME:** 5 MINUTES **COOK TIME:** 30 MINUTES

Berry-Coconut Breakfast Quinoa

Beth: This is a recipe I came up with when I was coaching high school cross-country, in an effort to get my athletes to start their day with an easily digestible carb that also contained a decent amount of protein. Cooking the quinoa in coconut milk adds a ton of extra flavor (and healthy fats), making this a well-balanced way to start your day. The topping possibilities are endless—fresh fruit, nut butter, coconut, maple syrup, or anything else your heart desires. Bonus: This quinoa tastes great hot or cold, so it's a perfect grab-and-go option on busy mornings (especially if you're sick of overnight oats).

One 13.5oz (400ml) can light coconut milk
3 tbsp pure maple syrup, or brown sugar
2 tbsp unsalted butter
1 tsp vanilla extract
½ tsp ground cinnamon
Pinch of kosher salt
1 cup quinoa
Fresh berries (like raspberries, blueberries, strawberries)

OPTIONAL TOPPINGS

Coconut flakes
Chopped nuts or seeds
Peanut or almond butter
Maple syrup or brown sugar

1. In a medium pot over medium heat, combine the coconut milk, maple syrup, butter, vanilla extract, cinnamon, salt, and ¼ cup water and whisk to combine. Add the quinoa and bring to a boil. Once boiling, reduce the heat to low and cover with a lid.
2. Cook the quinoa for 20 to 25 minutes, stirring a few times, until all the water has evaporated. Once ready, use a fork to fluff and stir.
3. To serve, divide the quinoa evenly between 4 bowls and serve with fresh berries and any toppings of your choice, such as coconut flakes, nuts or nut butter, or a drizzle of maple syrup. Serve this breakfast quinoa cold or warm.

Storage instructions: This will keep for 5 days in an airtight container in the refrigerator.

MAKES 16–18 | **PREP TIME:** 15 MINUTES **COOK TIME:** 30 MINUTES

Palačinky (Czech Crepes)

Lexi: My aunt Irena grew up in the Czech Republic, and she makes these palačinky for us every time we visit. They've become such a family tradition that this was one of the first recipes we knew we had to include in our cookbook! Palačinky are essentially the Czech version of crepes—a thin, delicate, eggy pancake with slightly crisp, golden-brown edges. Palačinky are slightly thicker than crepes, so they're easier to flip and much more forgiving, but for best results, you may want to invest in an inexpensive crepe pan. Otherwise, make sure you use a pan that has sloping sides for easier flipping. We typically fill ours with raspberry jam, Nutella, or cinnamon sugar and roll them up before digging in. Any flavor of jam or preserves will do, and if you're feeling fancy, you can top them off with whipped cream or a dusting of powdered sugar.

4 cups whole milk
2 large eggs
2 tsp vanilla extract
2½ cups all-purpose flour
6 tbsp powdered sugar
¼ tsp kosher salt
Butter or vegetable oil, for greasing

OPTIONAL TOPPINGS

Jam or preserves of choice
Nutella or nut butter
Powdered sugar or cinnamon sugar
Fresh berries

1. In a large bowl, whisk together the milk, eggs, and vanilla extract until no streaks remain. In a separate, medium bowl, stir together the flour, powdered sugar, and salt until evenly incorporated.
2. To the bowl with the wet ingredients, add the dry ingredients and whisk together until no lumps remain. Set the batter aside for 5 to 10 minutes, until it becomes the consistency of maple syrup.
3. Meanwhile, heat a 9-inch (23cm) crepe pan or shallow cast-iron pan over high heat. Lightly coat the pan with butter or vegetable oil and reduce the heat to medium.
4. Pour ⅓ cup of the batter into the hot pan. Working quickly, tilt the pan in circles or use a crepe spreader to spread the batter to the edges of the pan. Cook for about 1 minute, until the surface of the palačinky is dry and the edges begin to brown. Then, using a spatula, carefully flip the palačinky and cook for an additional minute, until lightly browned on the other side.
5. Transfer the palačinky to a plate and repeat the process until the batter runs out.
6. Layer each pancake with your choice of toppings. Roll it up and enjoy!

Make it dairy-free: Use full-fat oat milk in place of whole milk.

MAKES 8 | **PREP TIME:** 30 MINUTES, PLUS CHILLING TIME **COOK TIME:** 50 MINUTES

Blueberry Breakfast Tarts

Lexi: If you've been following us on social media for a while, you'll know that we love to recreate store-bought snacks from scratch. Pop-Tarts were a mainstay childhood breakfast for me, but the last time I tried them, they just weren't as good as I remembered. These homemade blueberry tarts, however, are a delightful treat. They're made with a crumbly, buttery crust (that doesn't taste like cardboard); a tart, lemony blueberry filling; and as much or as little frosting as your heart desires. Plus, that gorgeous bright purple hue is all natural! These tarts can be frozen (unfrosted) and reheated quickly in the oven when the craving strikes.

FOR THE DOUGH

2½ cups all-purpose flour, plus more for dusting
1 cup unsalted butter, chilled and cubed
4 tsp granulated sugar
2 tsp kosher salt

FOR THE FILLING

1lb (450g) blueberries
3 tbsp honey
1 tbsp freshly squeezed lemon juice
1 tsp lemon zest
1 large egg yolk, beaten

FOR THE GLAZE

1 cup powdered sugar
½ tsp freshly squeezed lemon juice
Sprinkles (optional)

1. To make the dough, in a food processor, combine the flour, butter, sugar, and salt and pulse a few times until the butter pieces are about the size of peas. Stream in ½ cup cold water, pulsing several more times, until a crumbly dough forms.
2. Transfer the dough to a large bowl or a lightly floured surface and gently knead it into a ball. Divide the dough in half, then wrap each half in plastic wrap and shape into a rectangle about 1 inch (2.5cm) thick. Place the dough in the refrigerator to chill for 2 hours.
3. To make the filling, to a medium saucepan over medium heat, add the blueberries, honey, lemon juice, and lemon zest. Using a potato masher, gently smash the blueberries, then reduce the heat to medium-low and let simmer for 20 to 25 minutes, stirring and mashing occasionally, until the mixture thickens. Remove from the heat and let cool completely. In a small bowl, reserve 2 tablespoons of the filling for the glaze. Set both aside.
4. Preheat the oven to 300°F (150°C) and line a sheet pan with parchment paper.
5. On a well-floured surface, roll one half of the dough into a large rectangle about ⅛ inch (3mm) thick, then trim it into a 14 x 10-inch (36 x 25cm) rectangle with straight edges. Cut the rectangle in half lengthwise, then cut each half into 4 rectangles of 3.5 x 5 inches (9 x 12cm). Repeat with the other half of the dough. In total, you will have 16 rectangles of dough.
6. Using a fork, dock several holes in the center of 8 of the rectangles (these will be the tops). Into the centers of the other 8 rectangles, spoon about 1½ tablespoons of the filling and spread into a thin layer, leaving a ⅓-inch (8mm) border around the edges.
7. Around the border of the filling, brush the beaten egg yolk, then place one of the docked rectangles on top, pressing down on the edges to secure. Using the tines of a fork, crimp and seal the edges of each tart. Transfer to the sheet pan, then repeat this process with the remaining dough.

8. Bake the tarts for 30 to 35 minutes, until very lightly browned on top and golden brown on the bottom. Carefully transfer to a cooling rack and let cool completely.
9. To make the glaze, to the small bowl with the reserved blueberry filling, add 1 tablespoon water, then strain it through a fine-mesh sieve into another small bowl, extracting as much blueberry juice as possible.
10. Add the powdered sugar and lemon juice to the blueberry juice and whisk until smooth. Spread as much of the glaze as you'd like over the cooled tarts, then top with sprinkles (if using).

Storage instructions: Keep the tarts in an airtight container for 3 days at room temperature or up to a week in the refrigerator.

MAKES 12 | **PREP TIME:** 30 MINUTES **COOK TIME:** 10 MINUTES

Baked Apple Cider Donuts

Fall in Michigan is synonymous with weekend trips to the cider mill. Every September, these seasonal businesses roar to life, drawing huge crowds seeking homemade cider donuts and fresh-pressed cider. Our baked donuts are for anyone who wants to capture the feeling of a crisp fall day without having to break out the fryer—or leave home. The crunchy cinnamon-sugar coating is a must!

FOR THE DONUTS

Cooking spray, for greasing
1½ cups apple cider
2¼ cups all-purpose flour
1½ tsp ground cinnamon
1 tsp baking powder
1 tsp baking soda
½ tsp ground ginger
¼ tsp ground nutmeg
¼ tsp kosher salt
½ cup light brown sugar, packed
⅓ cup whole milk
4 tbsp unsalted butter, melted
¼ cup unsweetened applesauce
¼ cup granulated sugar
1 tsp vanilla extract
1 tsp apple cider vinegar

FOR THE COATING

½ cup granulated sugar
1½ tsp ground cinnamon
2 tbsp unsalted butter, melted

1. Preheat the oven to 350°F (180°C). Lightly grease two 6-cavity donut pans with cooking spray.
2. To make the donuts, to a small saucepan over medium heat, add the apple cider and bring it to a simmer. Simmer for about 15 minutes, stirring occasionally, until the liquid reduces to ½ cup. Remove from the heat and set aside.
3. In a large bowl, whisk together the flour, cinnamon, baking powder, baking soda, ginger, nutmeg, and salt. Set aside.
4. In a separate large bowl, whisk together the brown sugar, milk, melted butter, applesauce, granulated sugar, vanilla extract, apple cider vinegar, and the reduced apple cider from step 2.
5. Using a spatula, stir the wet ingredients into the dry ingredients, mixing just until the batter comes together. Don't overmix. Transfer the batter to a gallon-size ziplock bag and snip off one corner of the bag with scissors. Into each cavity of the donut pan, pipe the batter about ¾ of the way to the top.
6. Bake for 10 to 11 minutes, until the tops are a light golden brown and a toothpick inserted into the center of a donut comes out clean. Let the donuts cool in the pans for 2 minutes, then flip over onto a cooling rack to remove the donuts.
7. To make the coating, in a shallow bowl, stir together the sugar and cinnamon.
8. Brush each donut lightly with the melted butter, then coat both sides in the cinnamon-sugar mixture. Serve warm.

Storage instructions: Let the donuts cool completely and transfer to an airtight container for up to 2 weeks.

Make it plant-based: Replace the whole milk and butter with nondairy milk and plant-based butter.

Make it gluten-free: Swap out the all-purpose flour for a gluten-free 1-to-1 or measure-for-measure flour.

MAKES 12 | PREP TIME: 30 MINUTES, PLUS RISING TIME COOK TIME: 30 MINUTES

Maple, Bourbon, and Pecan Sticky Buns

We both love a good cinnamon roll, but you know what's even better? A cinnamon roll that's doused in a sticky, sweet, bourbon-spiked pecan caramel! These may sound intimidating to make from scratch, but this recipe really doesn't require any more prep time than regular cinnamon rolls would. The caramel is very easy to make and comes together in just a few minutes, and otherwise, the most important part of this recipe is patience while the dough rises. If you want to get started ahead of time so you can have fresh rolls in the morning, follow the recipe up until the second rise. Cover the pan and refrigerate overnight, then let them rise at room temperature for about an hour before baking. These are a delicious treat for the holidays, or any weekend morning, best paired with a good cup of coffee.

FOR THE DOUGH

1 cup whole milk, warmed to 100–110°F (38–43°C)
1 packet or 2¼ tsp active dry yeast
⅓ cup granulated sugar, divided
4 tbsp unsalted butter, melted
1 large egg plus 1 large egg yolk, room temperature
½ tsp kosher salt
3½ cups all-purpose flour, plus more as needed
Cooking spray, for greasing

FOR THE CARAMEL

½ cup unsalted butter
¾ cup light brown sugar, packed
⅓ cup pure maple syrup
¼ cup heavy cream
¼ cup bourbon or whiskey
1 tsp vanilla extract
½ tsp kosher salt
1½ cups chopped toasted pecans

FOR THE FILLING

½ cup light brown sugar, packed
1 tbsp ground cinnamon
4 tbsp unsalted butter, softened

1. To make the dough, to the bowl of a stand mixer fitted with a dough hook, add the warm milk, yeast, and 1 tablespoon of the sugar. Let the mixture sit for 5 to 10 minutes, until the yeast is foamy.
2. Once foamy, add in the remaining 4 tablespoons and 1 teaspoon sugar, melted butter, egg and egg yolk, and salt and whisk until no streaks remain.
3. With the stand mixer on low speed, to the bowl, add the flour, mixing until a shaggy dough forms, then increase the speed to medium-high for 5 to 6 minutes, until the dough is smooth and elastic. If the dough sticks to the sides of the mixer, add 1 to 2 tablespoons of flour, 1 tablespoon at a time.
4. Transfer the dough to a large greased bowl and cover with a clean towel or plastic wrap. Let rise in a warm place for about 1½ hours, until doubled in size.
5. Grease a 9 x 13-inch (23 x 33cm) baking dish with cooking spray.
6. To make the caramel, to a medium saucepan over medium heat, add the butter and let melt. Stir in the brown sugar, maple syrup, and heavy cream. Bring to a simmer and cook for 2 to 3 minutes, stirring frequently, until slightly thickened. Remove from the heat and whisk in the bourbon, vanilla extract, and salt, then stir in the pecans. Pour the caramel into the greased baking dish and set aside.
7. To make the filling, in a small bowl, mix together the brown sugar and cinnamon.
8. Once the dough has doubled in size, punch it down and transfer to a lightly floured surface. Roll it into a 14 x 18-inch (36 x 46cm) rectangle. Spread the softened butter over the dough, all the way

to the edges, then sprinkle evenly with the cinnamon-sugar mixture. From the long side of the rectangle, roll the dough tightly into a log and cut into 12 rounds.

9. Evenly arrange the dough circles over the caramel in the baking dish. Cover with a clean towel or plastic wrap and let rise for 30 to 45 minutes, until puffy.
10. Preheat the oven to 350°F (180°C).
11. Bake for 30 to 35 minutes, until golden brown. If the tops brown too quickly, loosely tent with aluminum foil.
12. Let the buns cool in the pan for 10 minutes, then carefully flip them over onto a serving platter or a lined sheet pan while the caramel is still warm. Serve immediately and enjoy.

Snacks & Apps

MAKES ABOUT 50 | PREP TIME: 20 MINUTES, PLUS FREEZING TIME | COOK TIME: 55 MINUTES

Fruit-and-Nut Crackers

V

You know those fancy, artisanal fruit-and-nut crackers that cost an arm and a leg at the store? We're going to let you in on a little secret: You can make them at home for a fraction of the price! This is the perfect recipe to make when you have half-finished bags of dried fruit and nuts that have been sitting in your pantry for way too long. The end result is a flavorful, crisp, beautiful cracker that's perfect for charcuterie boards and is prized loot for any pantry raider (like Dad). You can tightly wrap and freeze the baked loaves for several months, so you can always have freshly baked crackers within 30 minutes.

- ¾ cup chopped dried fruit (apricots, figs, dates, raisins, cherries, etc.)
- ¾ cup chopped nuts or seeds (pecans, pumpkin seeds, pistachios, walnuts, almonds, sunflower seeds, etc.)
- ½ cup all-purpose flour
- ½ cup whole-wheat flour
- 1 tbsp finely chopped rosemary, or 1 tsp dried rosemary
- 1 tbsp finely chopped thyme, or 1 tsp dried thyme
- 1 tbsp orange zest
- 1½ tsp kosher salt
- 1 tsp baking soda
- ½ tsp ground cinnamon
- ⅛ tsp ground nutmeg
- ⅛ tsp ground black pepper
- 1 cup milk of choice
- ¼ cup honey

1. Preheat the oven to 350°F (180°C). Line 2 mini loaf pans (5½ x 3¼ inches / 13 x 8cm) with parchment paper.
2. To a large bowl, add the dried fruit, nuts, all-purpose flour, whole-wheat flour, rosemary, thyme, orange zest, salt, baking soda, cinnamon, nutmeg, and pepper and stir until well combined. Mix in the milk and honey until no streaks of honey remain.
3. Divide the batter equally between the 2 mini loaf pans. Bake for 25 to 28 minutes, until a toothpick inserted into the center comes out clean.
4. Let the loaves cool to room temperature in the pan, then remove, wrap each loaf tightly in plastic wrap, and freeze for at least 3 hours (or up to 3 months).
5. Preheat the oven to 300°F (150°C). Line 2 sheet pans with parchment paper.
6. Remove the loaves from the freezer and using a serrated knife, slice the crackers into ⅛-inch (3mm) slices. Transfer the crackers to the sheet pans.
7. Bake for 12 minutes, then carefully flip each cracker over and bake for another 12 minutes. Flip the crackers over one more time and cook for 4 to 8 minutes, until they are golden brown and feel mostly dry to the touch. Let them cool on the pan; the crackers will continue to crisp up as they cool. Once fully cooled, store in an airtight container at room temperature for up to 5 days.

Make it plant-based: Use oat milk and maple syrup or agave instead of honey.

MAKES 175–200 | **PREP TIME: 30 MINUTES** **COOK TIME: 20 MINUTES**

Five-Ingredient White Cheddar Crackers

Cheesy, crispy, and salty, these easy white cheddar crackers taste exactly like the store-bought versions we all know and love. We first shared this recipe on Instagram a few years ago, and it's been a huge hit ever since. These crackers are a breeze to make, only require a few very basic ingredients, and taste truly incredible for how simple they are. Our only issue with this recipe is that it's way too easy to eat the entire batch in one sitting. Any cheddar works, but shred it from a block versus purchasing pre-shredded cheese, which has anti-caking agents that prevent it from incorporating into the dough as well.

8oz (225g) extra-sharp white cheddar cheese, finely shredded
1 cup all-purpose flour, plus more for dusting
½ tsp kosher salt, plus more to top
4 tbsp unsalted butter
2 tbsp whole milk

1. Preheat the oven to 325°F (165°C). Line 2 sheet pans with parchment paper.
2. To the bowl of a food processor, add the cheese, flour, and salt and pulse several times until the cheese has broken down into tiny bits. Add the butter and pulse a few more times, until the dough is crumbly. Add the milk, then pulse several more times, until the dough comes together when you press it between two fingers.
3. Transfer the dough to a lightly floured surface. Roll into a large rectangle as thinly as possible. You should be able to just begin to see your rolling surface through the thin dough. We go even thinner than ⅛ inch (3mm) thick, as the crackers puff up quite a bit when baking.
4. Using a knife, a pizza cutter, or a fluted pastry wheel, trim the edges of the dough, then slice into 1-inch (2.5cm) squares. Using the flat end of a skewer, poke a hole all the way through the center of each cracker. With a small spatula, transfer the crackers to the prepared sheet pans, making sure the crackers are not touching. Sprinkle with more salt to taste.
5. Bake for 17 to 20 minutes, until the bottom of each cracker is a deep golden brown. If the crackers are too light, they will not be very crisp. Let cool in the pan completely before enjoying.

Storage instructions: Store the crackers in an airtight container at room temperature for up to 1 week.

SERVES 6–8 | PREP TIME: 35 MINUTES COOK TIME: 45 MINUTES

Roasted Beet and Feta Dip

This vibrant beet and feta dip is an easy and impressive appetizer to whip up for any occasion! It's super creamy, tangy, and perfect for pairing with a rainbow of crunchy crudités, toasted baguette, or pita chips. We like to top ours with a swirl of olive oil and za'atar for extra flavor.

1 large red beet (about 8oz / 225g), peeled and diced into 1-inch (2.5cm) cubes
2 large garlic cloves
3 tbsp olive oil, divided, plus more to garnish
1½ tsp finely chopped oregano
1 tsp finely chopped thyme
¼ tsp kosher salt, plus more to taste
¼ tsp ground black pepper, plus more to taste
1 tbsp freshly squeezed lemon juice
1 tsp lemon zest
8oz (225g) feta cheese
5oz (140g) plain Greek yogurt
1 tsp za'atar, to garnish
Chopped parsley, to garnish (optional)

1. Preheat the oven to 400°F (200°C).
2. In the center of a large square of aluminum foil, place the diced beets and garlic cloves. Drizzle with 1 tablespoon of the olive oil and sprinkle with the oregano, thyme, salt, and pepper. Gently toss to coat, then wrap the aluminum foil tightly around the beets and garlic.
3. Transfer to a small sheet pan and roast for about 45 minutes, until the beets are fork tender. Remove from the oven and carefully open the aluminum foil. Let cool for 15 minutes.
4. To a food processor or a blender, add the beets, garlic, lemon juice, lemon zest, and the remaining 2 tablespoons olive oil. Pulse several times, until the beets are very finely chopped. Scrape down the sides of the food processor, then blend for 30 seconds until the beets are smooth.
5. Add in the feta and yogurt and continue blending until smooth and well combined, scraping down the sides of the food processor as needed. Season with additional salt and pepper to taste.
6. Serve topped with a drizzle of olive oil, za'atar, and parsley (if using).

SERVES 8 | PREP TIME: 30 MINUTES

Loaded Greek Salad Hummus

We took two of our all-time favorite recipes and combined them into one satisfying dish: Greek salad hummus! The vegetables are finely chopped so they're easy to scoop with pita chips. You can substitute store-bought hummus if you're short on time, but homemade always tastes brighter and fresher. Both components can be made ahead of time—just store them separately for up to 1 day until right before serving.

FOR THE GREEK SALAD

¾ cup diced baby cucumber
¾ cup quartered cherry tomatoes
¼ cup roughly chopped pitted kalamata olives
3 tbsp finely chopped pepperoncini
2 tbsp finely diced red onion
2 tbsp finely chopped parsley
1 tbsp finely chopped mint
2 tbsp olive oil
½ tbsp freshly squeezed lemon juice
Salt and ground black pepper, to taste
⅓ cup crumbled feta cheese, divided

FOR THE HUMMUS

One 15½oz (440g) can chickpeas, drained with ¼ cup canning liquid reserved
¼ cup tahini
3 tbsp freshly squeezed lemon juice
2 garlic cloves
½ tsp kosher salt, plus more to taste
½ tsp ground cumin
¼ cup olive oil
Pita bread or pita chips, to serve

1. To make the Greek salad, in a medium bowl, stir together the cucumber, tomatoes, olives, pepperoncini, onion, parsley, and mint.
2. In a small bowl, whisk together the olive oil and lemon juice, then pour over the salad. Season with salt and pepper to taste and add half of the feta cheese. Stir everything together until well coated, then set aside.
3. To make the hummus, to a food processor or blender, add the chickpeas and 3 tablespoons of the reserved liquid, tahini, lemon juice, garlic cloves, salt, and cumin. Blend until the hummus is mostly smooth, then slowly stream in the olive oil while continuing to blend, until completely smooth. If needed for consistency, add the remaining 1 tablespoon of canning liquid from the chickpeas. Taste and adjust the salt as desired.
4. On a small platter or in a shallow bowl, spread the hummus, then use a slotted spoon to add the salad over top, leaving any excess dressing from the salad behind. Garnish with the remaining feta cheese before serving with pita bread or pita chips.

Make it plant-based: Leave out the feta or substitute with your favorite plant-based alternative.

STAUB
STAUB

SERVES 8–10 | PREP TIME: 15 MINUTES COOK TIME: 35 MINUTES

Cheesy Corn Poblano Dip

GF

With chorizo, poblano pepper, corn, and plenty of cheese, this warm dip just screams "game day." It's a little spicy, a whole lot of cheesy, and absolutely packed with flavor in every bite. Fresh corn is great if it's in season, but for the rest of the year, frozen is perfectly fine (and honestly, much easier). Make sure to grab a bag of sturdy tortilla or pita chips for dipping!

8oz (225g) ground chorizo
¾ cup diced poblano pepper, seeds removed
½ small yellow onion, diced
One 4oz (115g) can mild diced green chiles
10oz (285g) frozen sweet corn
2 tbsp finely chopped cilantro
¾ tsp dried oregano
½ tsp smoked paprika
¼ tsp ground cumin
¼ tsp garlic powder
¼ tsp kosher salt
2 cups shredded sharp cheddar cheese, divided
4oz (115g) cream cheese, softened
¼ cup sour cream
Chopped green onions and/or cilantro, to garnish
Tortilla or pita chips, to serve

1. Preheat the oven to 425°F (220°C).
2. To a 10-inch (25cm) cast-iron skillet over medium heat, add the chorizo and cook for about 7 minutes, stirring often, until browned. Remove from the skillet with a slotted spoon, leaving the fat in the pan, and transfer to a plate. Set aside.
3. To the same skillet, add the poblano pepper, onion, and green chiles. Cook, stirring often, for 5 minutes, until the onion is softened.
4. Stir in the corn, cilantro, oregano, paprika, cumin, garlic powder, and salt and continue cooking for 5 minutes, stirring occasionally, until the corn is thawed and softened. Remove from the heat, then add in ¾ cup of the shredded cheddar cheese, followed by the cream cheese and sour cream, stirring until the cream cheese is melted and fully incorporated.
5. Add in the cooked chorizo, then with a spatula, smooth the dip into an even layer in the skillet. Top with the remaining 1¼ cups cheddar cheese.
6. Bake for about 15 minutes, until the dip is bubbling and the cheese has melted. Let cool for 10 minutes before garnishing with the green onions and/or cilantro and serving with tortilla chips.

Make it vegetarian: Use your favorite plant-based spicy sausage alternative in place of chorizo.

MAKES 16 | PREP TIME: 15 MINUTES COOK TIME: 15 MINUTES

Figs in a Blanket

Aka fresh figs stuffed with goat cheese, wrapped in prosciutto, and baked until crispy, melty, and cheesy! We finish them off with a drizzle of honey and/or balsamic glaze, plus a sprinkle of fresh thyme, but they're also delicious plain, straight out of the oven. You get salty, sweet, and tangy in every bite. There are two seasons for fresh figs in the US: the first is in June, and the second is from August to October, so we most often make these as an early fall appetizer. Black Mission or Brown Turkey are our figs of choice, and both are commonly found in most stores when in season. Larger figs are definitely better so there's more surface area. You'll need to scoop out a little bit of the interior to add in the goat cheese, but don't get rid of it! We add ours to a bowl of yogurt, granola, and honey the next morning.

FOR THE FIGS

8 large fresh figs, sliced in half lengthwise
⅓ cup goat cheese
8 slices prosciutto, sliced in half lengthwise

FOR SERVING

Honey
Balsamic glaze
Chopped thyme (optional)
Black pepper (optional)

1. Preheat the oven to 375°F (190°C).
2. Using a small spoon (or a melon baller), scoop out a small cavity in the center of each fig half (a little less than 1 teaspoon). Fill each cavity with about 1 teaspoon of goat cheese. Use a bit less for smaller figs, since the filling will ooze out slightly in the oven.
3. Wrap each fig half tightly with the prosciutto. On a nonstick sheet pan, place the figs flat-side down. (You don't need to use parchment paper.)
4. Bake for about 15 minutes (or 12 minutes for small figs), until the prosciutto is crispy on the bottom and the figs are soft. Let cool for a few minutes on the pan, then remove with a spatula and transfer to a plate or serving platter.
5. Top the stuffed figs with a drizzle of honey and balsamic glaze, a sprinkle of fresh thyme (if using), and black pepper (if using). Enjoy warm.

MAKES 48 | PREP TIME: 40 MINUTES COOK TIME: 30 MINUTES

Baked Strawberry-Balsamic Brie Bites

V

This is a beautiful two-bite summer appetizer that comes together quickly. Strawberries and balsamic vinegar are a match made in heaven, especially paired with melty brie and baked inside a crispy puff pastry boat. Yum! To make prep even faster, you can shortcut this recipe by using your favorite store-bought strawberry jam with a bit of balsamic vinegar mixed in. For a fall and winter pairing that's great for holiday entertaining, swap the strawberries with fresh or frozen cranberries, and basil with chopped thyme. Pro tip: To make the brie easier to slice, place it in the freezer for 15 to 20 minutes before cutting. We like to throw it in the freezer while we make the strawberry jam!

FOR THE BRIE BITES

- Nonstick spray, for greasing
- All-purpose flour, for dusting
- One 17.3oz (490g) box puff pastry, thawed (2 sheets)
- One 8oz (225g) wheel of brie, sliced into 1-inch (2.5cm) squares about ¼ inch (5mm) thick
- 2 tbsp finely chopped basil
- 2 tbsp chopped toasted pecans

FOR THE JAM

- 1lb (450g) strawberries, diced into ½-inch (1cm) pieces
- 2 tbsp honey
- 1½ tbsp balsamic vinegar
- ¼ tsp kosher salt
- ¼ tsp ground black pepper
- ½ tsp vanilla extract

1. Preheat the oven to 400°F (200°C). Grease two 24-cup mini muffin tins with nonstick spray.
2. To make the jam, in a small pot, combine the strawberries, honey, balsamic vinegar, salt, and pepper. Cook over medium heat, stirring occasionally, until the mixture starts to bubble, then reduce the heat to medium-low.
3. Simmer for 10 to 12 minutes, stirring occasionally and mashing the berries with the back of a spoon, until the jam starts to thicken. Remove from the heat, then stir in the vanilla extract and set aside to cool.
4. To make the brie bites, on a floured surface, roll a sheet of puff pastry into a 12.5-inch (32cm) square. Using a pizza cutter or a knife, cut into 2.5-inch (6.4cm) squares to make 24 in total. Repeat this process with the other sheet of puff pastry, to yield 48 squares.
5. Press each puff pastry square into a cavity of the greased mini muffin tins. Add a slice of brie over each, then top with about 1 teaspoon of the strawberry jam.
6. Bake for 18 to 20 minutes, until the pastry is lightly browned and puffed up. Let cool in the muffin tin for about 5 minutes, then run a knife around the edges of the puff pastries to release them from the pan. Transfer to a serving platter.
7. Garnish with the basil and pecans and serve warm.

MAKES 16 | **PREP TIME:** 20 MINUTES, PLUS COOLING TIME **COOK TIME:** 40 MINUTES

Spinach and Artichoke Puff Pastry Bites

This is an appetizer recipe we keep coming back to for holidays and entertaining. It combines a tried-and-true appetizer combination—spinach and artichoke—with plenty of cheese; pancetta or bacon for extra flavor; and crispy, golden-brown puff pastry. For best results with the puff pastry, let it thaw overnight in the refrigerator. Keep it cold while you assemble everything, and if it gets too warm, pop the unbaked bites in the refrigerator for 15 to 30 minutes before baking. Cold puff pastry means the butter will melt more slowly when it bakes, which creates those beautiful, flaky layers. Entertaining tip: This is the perfect recipe to assemble a day ahead of time—just cover and refrigerate the unbaked squares until you're ready to bake!

2oz (60g) pancetta or bacon, diced into ¼-inch (5mm) pieces
½ cup minced shallots
2 garlic cloves, minced
5oz (140g) spinach, chopped
7oz (200g) water-packed artichokes, drained and chopped
2 tbsp chopped parsley
½ tsp dried oregano
¼ tsp kosher salt
¼ tsp ground black pepper
⅔ cup crumbled feta cheese
⅔ cup shredded mozzarella cheese
¼ cup grated Parmesan, plus more for topping
Large egg, white and yolk separated
All-purpose flour, for dusting
One 17.3oz (490g) box puff pastry, thawed (2 sheets)
Sesame seeds, to garnish (optional)

1. Position a rack in the middle of the oven. Preheat to 375°F (190°C). Line a sheet pan with parchment paper.
2. To a medium skillet over medium heat, add the pancetta and cook, stirring frequently, for 2 to 3 minutes, until the fat starts to render—it will liquify and start to cover the bottom of the pan. Then, add the shallots and continue cooking and stirring for another 2 to 3 minutes, until the shallots are softened and translucent. Add the garlic and cook for 1 minute, until fragrant.
3. Add the spinach, artichokes, parsley, oregano, salt, and pepper and cook for 3 to 5 minutes, until the spinach is wilted. Transfer the filling to a medium bowl and place in the refrigerator for about 10 minutes to cool.
4. Remove the filling from the fridge and add the feta, mozzarella, Parmesan, and egg white and stir until evenly incorporated. Set aside.
5. Lightly dust a clean work surface and roll out each sheet of puff pastry into a 12-inch (30cm) square. Add more flour to your work surface as necessary to prevent sticking.
6. In a small bowl, whisk together the egg yolk with 1 teaspoon of water.
7. On top of one of the puff pastry squares, spread the filling in an even layer, leaving a small border around the edges to prevent spillage when cutting. Place the other puff pastry square on top and brush it with the egg wash.
8. Using a pizza cutter or a sharp knife, cut the puff pastry into sixteen 3-inch (7.5cm) squares. Sprinkle the top of each with Parmesan and sesame seeds (if using). Transfer to the sheet pan, spacing the bites slightly apart.
9. Bake on the middle rack for about 30 minutes, until golden brown. Let cool for 5 to 10 minutes in the pan and enjoy hot.

MAKES ABOUT 40 | **PREP TIME:** 5 MINUTES, PLUS CHILLING TIME **COOK TIME:** 35 MINUTES

GF 

Crispy Polenta Bites
with Pesto, Burrata, and Tomatoes

Beth: Think of these as little crostini bites, but with a square of crispy, cheesy polenta in place of the bread. If I'm being totally honest, as much as I love the versatility and ease of crostini, sometimes the toasted bread is just so crunchy that it's not enjoyable to eat. That's why we swapped the rock-hard bread for baked polenta! You can make the polenta squares 3 to 4 days ahead of time and assemble the toppings just before serving. Pesto, burrata, and cherry tomatoes are easy, refreshing options for summer, but don't stop there. Try these bites with whipped feta, peaches, basil, and honey or with sour cream, smoked salmon, capers, and dill.

FOR THE POLENTA SQUARES

2 cups vegetable broth
1½ cups whole milk
1½ cups polenta
1 tsp kosher salt
¾ tsp garlic powder
½ tsp ground black pepper
¼ cup grated Parmesan or pecorino romano
3 tbsp unsalted butter
2–3 tbsp olive oil, for brushing

FOR SERVING

1 cup Easy Homemade Pesto (page 252) or store-bought
8oz (225g) burrata cheese
20 cherry tomatoes, halved
Cracked black pepper, to taste
Olive oil

1. To make the polenta squares, in a medium saucepan over high heat, combine the vegetable broth and whole milk. Bring to a boil, then reduce the heat to medium-low and slowly whisk in the polenta until no dry clumps remain. Then whisk in the salt, garlic powder, and pepper until evenly incorporated. Cover with a lid and cook over low heat for 10 minutes, stirring occasionally, until the polenta starts to thicken and looks less gritty.
2. Add the cheese and butter and cook, stirring, until the butter is melted and the cheese has started to melt. Then let simmer, covered, for another 5 to 10 minutes, until the polenta is thick and begins to pull away from the sides of the pan.
3. Meanwhile, line a 13 x 18-inch (33 x 46cm) sheet pan with parchment paper.
4. Once the polenta is done, quickly pour it out onto the sheet pan and, using a spatula, spread it into an even, smooth layer, about ¼-inch (5mm) thick. Cover loosely with plastic wrap and refrigerate for at least 2 hours or overnight to set.
5. Preheat the oven to 450°F (230°C).
6. Onto a cutting board, carefully flip out the chilled polenta. Slice into 2-inch (5cm) squares. Line another sheet pan with parchment paper.
7. Transfer the polenta squares to the parchment-lined sheet pan, leaving some space between each, and brush the tops lightly with olive oil.
8. Bake for 10 to 12 minutes, until the squares are crispy and the edges have begun to brown. Remove from the oven and using a spatula, flip the squares over. Brush again with the olive oil and return to the oven for 10 to 12 minutes, until the polenta is golden brown around the edges.
9. Remove from the oven and transfer the polenta squares to a wire rack to cool for 15 to 20 minutes, until crispy and no longer hot to the touch.
10. Top each polenta square with 1 teaspoon of pesto, a small piece of burrata, and a cherry tomato half. Add black pepper to taste and a drizzle of olive oil.

MAKES ABOUT 30 | PREP TIME: 10 MINUTES COOK TIME: 40 MINUTES

Brent's Lemon Pepper Wings

Lexi: My husband, Brent, developed this recipe a few years ago, and it has been on repeat in our house ever since, highly demanded by family and friends. We always joke that if we had a restaurant, these would be one of the bestsellers. The wings are oven-baked on a wire rack until super crispy and golden brown, then tossed in a very buttery, very lemony sauce that's truly lick-your-fingers good. Every brand of lemon pepper seasoning tastes a little different—our consistent favorite is Lawry's. You can adjust the seasoning to taste if you prefer another brand. This is the perfect recipe to file away for game day, or any time you need a crowd-pleasing app!

3lb (1.35kg) split or party chicken wings (about 32 wings and drumettes total)
¼ cup avocado or olive oil
¾ cup unsalted butter
¼ cup lemon pepper seasoning
2 tbsp freshly squeezed lemon juice
2 tsp lemon zest

1. Preheat the oven to 425°F (220°C). Arrange a wire cooling rack atop a rimmed sheet pan lined with aluminum foil.
2. In a large bowl, combine the wings and avocado oil, then toss until the wings are coated.
3. On the wire cooling rack, place the wings meatier-side up. They can be close together.
4. Bake for 40 to 45 minutes (bigger wings may take longer), until the wings are light brown and the skin is crispy to the touch.
5. About 10 minutes before the wings are done cooking, in a small saucepan over medium-low heat, melt the butter, stirring occasionally. Add the lemon pepper seasoning and lemon juice, and whisk until no dry streaks remain.
6. Remove the wings from the oven and carefully transfer them to a large bowl. Pour the butter mixture over the wings, and toss to evenly coat.
7. Sprinkle the lemon zest on top and toss once or twice again. Serve immediately.

SERVES 2–4 | **PREP TIME:** 15 MINUTES **COOK TIME:** 10 MINUTES

Grilled Flatbread

with Pesto Ricotta, Melon, and Prosciutto

Melon and prosciutto paired together is a classic Italian summer appetizer that's salty, sweet, and refreshing all in one. They're extra delicious atop a grilled flatbread and a bed of our two-ingredient pesto ricotta, with some peppery arugula, a drizzle of good-quality olive oil, a touch of honey, and flaky salt and pepper to finish it off. Grilling your bread may sound intimidating, but it's actually far easier than using the oven—there's no fussing with rack positioning, it doesn't have to be perfectly shaped, and it only takes a few minutes to cook! Make sure to oil the grill grates before cooking and use enough flour when stretching the pizza dough so it's easy to move around. We almost always purchase fresh pizza dough from our local specialty grocery store, which is way easier than making it from scratch!

Avocado oil or olive oil, for greasing
All-purpose flour, for dusting
10oz (285g) pizza dough
½ cup whole-milk ricotta
2 tbsp Easy Homemade Pesto (page 252) or store-bought
3oz (85g) prosciutto
10–12 slices of cantaloupe, about 2 inches (5cm) thick
1 cup (20g) arugula, lightly packed
2 tbsp chiffonade basil (see note)
Olive oil, to garnish
Honey, to garnish
Flaky salt and ground black pepper, to taste

1. Preheat the grill to medium-high heat (400 to 450°F / 200 to 230°C). Drizzle some avocado oil on a paper towel. Using a pair of tongs, rub the oiled paper towel onto the grill grates.
2. On a well-floured surface, press and stretch the pizza dough into a rectangle or oval, about 14 x 8 inches (36 x 20cm). Using a fork, dock the dough all over to prevent it from puffing up too much on the grill.
3. Carefully transfer the dough to the preheated grill. This is easiest to do on a well-floured surface. We typically slide the dough onto a large cutting board and then onto the grill. Cook for about 5 minutes on one side, until the dough easily releases from the grill and has distinct grill marks. Using tongs, carefully flip the flatbread and cook for another 5 minutes, until grill marks have formed and the bread is cooked through. Remove from the grill and set aside to cool for 10 minutes.
4. In a small bowl, mix the ricotta and pesto until no large streaks remain. Spread the ricotta-pesto mixture on top of the cooled bread, leaving a small border around the edges.
5. Arrange the prosciutto and cantaloupe on top, then scatter with the arugula and basil. Drizzle with the olive oil and honey, and sprinkle with flaky salt and black pepper to taste. Cut into strips or slices and enjoy right away.

Note: To chiffonade basil, stack several basil leaves atop one another. Roll the leaves lengthwise into a tight cylinder, then slice crosswise into thin strips.

SERVES 6–8 | **PREP TIME:** 10 MINUTES **COOK TIME:** 45 MINUTES

Loaded Potato Wedge Nachos

Lexi: Every Super Bowl since I can remember, my dad has made sheet-pan "super" nachos, which are essentially regular nachos loaded up with lots of ground beef, melty cheese, beans, olives, and whatever else we felt like adding. These are a nod to our family tradition, but with crispy potato wedges in place of the tortilla chips! The wedges hold up better with heavy toppings and don't get soggy or too dry (common issues with regular nachos). Homemade wedges are definitely worth the effort, but if you're in a pinch, you could absolutely use your favorite frozen potato wedges instead (we like the Alexia brand).

4–5 medium Russet potatoes, about 3lb (1.35kg) in total, sliced into wedges 1 inch (2.5cm) thick
3½ tsp chili powder, divided
2¼ tsp kosher salt, divided
1¼ tsp garlic powder, divided
3 tbsp avocado or vegetable oil
1lb (450g) 80% lean ground beef
¾ tsp dried oregano
½ tsp ground cumin
½ tsp ground coriander
¼ tsp smoked paprika
3 cups shredded Mexican-style cheese blend

OPTIONAL TOPPINGS

2 Roma tomatoes, diced (or your favorite salsa)
1 avocado, diced
3–4 radishes, thinly sliced
¼ cup sour cream or crema
Finely chopped cilantro

1. Preheat the oven to 450°F (230°C).
2. Bring a large pot of salted water to a boil. Add the potato wedges, then reduce the heat slightly and let simmer for about 5 minutes, until the potatoes are just slightly softened. Using a slotted spoon, transfer the potatoes to a clean dish towel on a flat surface to drain for a few minutes. Set aside.
3. In a small bowl, combine 2 teaspoons of the chili powder, 1½ teaspoons of the salt, and ¾ teaspoon of the garlic powder, and stir until evenly incorporated.
4. To a large bowl, add the parcooked potatoes and drizzle with the oil. Sprinkle the seasoning mixture over the potatoes and toss gently to evenly coat.
5. Spread the wedges out on a sheet pan covered with parchment paper in a single layer. Bake for 22 to 25 minutes, flipping halfway through, until the potatoes are lightly browned and crispy. Set aside on the sheet pan.
6. While the wedges bake, heat a large skillet over medium-high heat. Add in the ground beef and cook for 7 to 8 minutes, using a wooden spoon to break up chunks into smaller pieces, until the beef is browned, crispy, and cooked through. Stir in the remaining 1½ teaspoons chili powder, ¾ teaspoon salt, ½ teaspoon garlic powder, as well as the oregano, cumin, coriander, and paprika, and continue cooking for 1 minute, stirring continuously until no dry spices remain.
7. Sprinkle about 1 cup of the shredded cheese over the potatoes, then spread an even layer of the cooked ground beef over the cheese, and finish with a final layer of the remaining cheese atop the ground beef. Return to the oven and bake for about 10 minutes, until the cheese is melted.
8. Add your toppings of choice and serve immediately.

Make it plant-based: If you want to make this fully plant-based, we suggest using a plant-based nacho-cheese sauce instead of shredded plant-based cheese.

Make it vegetarian: Try these with your favorite plant-based ground beef alternative or add a can of black beans instead.

Soups

SERVES 4-5 | PREP TIME: 20 MINUTES COOK TIME: 50 MINUTES

Super Green Sheet-Pan Soup

with Pesto Grilled Cheese Croutons

The beauty of this soup is that it's hands-off, and it's a fantastic way to get in several servings of vegetables without even noticing. Just toss everything onto one big sheet pan, and leave it to roast for about a half hour before adding it to a blender with warmed broth. You can customize it with just about any vegetables you have on hand, but don't skip the potatoes and cauliflower, since they provide the body of the soup. This dish is super creamy, super green, and surprisingly delicious (and not *too* green tasting, despite the color). The real star of the show is the pesto grilled cheese croutons. Of course, you can always just make a regular grilled cheese and dip it right in the soup, but cutting it up into croutons is extra fun.

FOR THE SOUP

1 small head of garlic, about 8 cloves
3 tbsp olive oil, divided
1 large leek, sliced
8oz (225g) cauliflower, chopped
6oz (175g) broccoli, chopped
1 medium-large zucchini, diced
12oz (350g) yellow potatoes, peeled and diced
1½ tsp kosher salt
1 tsp dried oregano
½ tsp ground black pepper
3 cups vegetable broth
1 cup frozen peas
2 cups baby spinach, packed
3 tbsp parsley
3 tbsp freshly squeezed lemon juice
¼ tsp red pepper flakes (optional)

FOR THE CROUTONS

2 tbsp unsalted butter
4 slices of sourdough bread
6 slices of pepper jack cheese
4 tbsp Easy Homemade Pesto (page 252) or store-bought

1. Preheat the oven to 400°F (200°C).
2. Slice off the top of the head of garlic to expose the cloves. Drizzle 1 teaspoon of the olive oil over it, then wrap it in a small piece of aluminum foil. Place it in the corner of a large sheet pan.
3. To the same sheet pan, add the leek, cauliflower, broccoli, zucchini, and potatoes. Drizzle with the remaining olive oil and sprinkle with the salt, oregano, and pepper. Using a spatula or your hands, mix to coat the vegetables evenly.
4. Roast for 30 to 35 minutes, stirring once halfway through, until all the vegetables are fork tender.
5. Meanwhile, in a medium skillet over low heat, melt half of the butter. Place 2 slices of the bread down and cook for about 8 minutes, until golden brown.
6. Flip the bread over, then top one with 3 slices of the cheese. Spread 2 tablespoons of the pesto on top, then place the other slice of bread toasted-side down over the pesto. Cover with a lid and cook for about 5 minutes, until the bottom is golden brown, then flip and continue cooking for another 5 minutes, until the other side is golden brown and the cheese is melted. Remove from the heat and repeat to make a second sandwich. Transfer the grilled cheeses to a cutting board and slice into 1-inch (2.5cm) cubes. Set aside.
7. About 10 minutes before the vegetables are done roasting, in a small pot over medium heat, combine the broth and peas and bring to a simmer, then reduce the heat to low and let cook for 10 minutes, until the peas are thawed and tender and the broth is steaming hot.

8. When the vegetables are done roasting, carefully open the foil-wrapped garlic and let cool for a few minutes. To a blender, add the hot broth, peas, and the roasted vegetables, squeeze in the garlic cloves, then add the spinach, parsley, lemon juice, and red pepper flakes (if using). You may need to work in batches—be sure only to fill your blender halfway. Blend for about 1 minute, until completely smooth, being sure to crack the blender lid away from you to let steam escape.
9. Pour the soup into bowls and serve hot with the grilled cheese croutons scattered on top.

STAUB

SERVES 4–8 | PREP TIME: 15 MINUTES COOK TIME: 1 HOUR 15 MINUTES

V

French Leek and Greens Soup

This recipe is a play on the classic French onion soup, but with a lighter flavor profile that's perfect for spring. Leeks are milder and slightly sweeter than regular onions, so instead of beef broth and brandy or sherry, we opt for vegetable broth and a dry white wine to add depth of flavor. Spinach (or kale), fresh parsley, and lemon juice lighten the dish up even further. But of course, we kept the best part—the crusty, cheesy broiled bread topping. Shredded Gruyère is our cheese of choice, but you can also use a sharp white cheddar, Swiss, or provolone. Since these go under the broiler, make sure your bowls or crocks are oven safe. Tip: You can use the whole leek in this recipe, including the dark green parts.

- ¼ cup olive oil, plus more for brushing on bread
- 3–4 large leeks, halved lengthwise and thinly sliced
- 1 tbsp chopped thyme, plus more to garnish
- 1½ tsp kosher salt
- ¼ tsp ground black pepper, plus more to taste
- 3 garlic cloves, minced
- ⅓ cup dry white wine
- 6 cups vegetable broth, divided
- 2 tbsp all-purpose flour
- 2 bay leaves
- 1 baguette, sliced into 1-inch (2.5cm) slices
- 2 cups spinach or kale, packed and chopped (optional)
- ¼ cup chopped parsley
- 2 tbsp unsalted butter
- 1½ tbsp freshly squeezed lemon juice
- ¾ cup shredded Gruyère cheese

1. Preheat the oven to 375°F (190°C).
2. To a large pot over medium heat, add the oil. Once the oil is hot and shimmers or ripples slightly, add in the leeks, thyme, salt, and pepper. Cook, stirring occasionally, for about 30 minutes, until the leeks are softened and caramelized. If they start to burn, reduce the heat to low.
3. Add the minced garlic and cook for 2 to 3 minutes, stirring often, until fragrant. Pour in the white wine to deglaze the pan, stirring to scrape up any browned bits, and cook for another 2 to 3 minutes, until the wine has mostly evaporated.
4. In a small bowl, whisk together 1 cup of the broth with the flour until no lumps remain. Add the flour mixture to the pot along with the remaining 5 cups broth and the bay leaves and stir to combine. Increase the heat to high and bring the soup to a boil. Once boiling, reduce the heat to medium-low, cover with a lid, and simmer for 20 minutes, stirring occasionally, until slightly thickened.
5. Meanwhile, on a sheet pan, spread out the baguette slices and brush both sides lightly with olive oil. Bake for 6 to 8 minutes, until the bread is just lightly browned around the edges. Let cool on the pan.
6. Once the soup has simmered for 20 minutes, add the spinach (if using), parsley, butter, and lemon juice and continue cooking for 2 to 3 minutes, until the spinach is wilted.
7. Position a rack at the top of the oven and set it to broil. On a sturdy sheet pan, place 4 large oven-safe bowls or 8 smaller oven-safe crocks or ramekins.
8. Ladle the soup into the bowls or crocks. Top each with 1 or 2 baguette slices, then sprinkle with a generous amount of shredded cheese. Place on the top rack of the oven and broil for 2 to 4 minutes, until the cheese is bubbly and melted. Keep a close eye, as they can burn quickly under the broiler.
9. Let cool for a few minutes before serving hot, garnished with more thyme. The bowls will be very hot, so be careful!

SERVES 4 | PREP TIME: 15 MINUTES

Cucumber, Basil, and Avocado Gazpacho

When we say this recipe is easy, we really mean it. There's almost no prep work required—just roughly chop the vegetables, then toss everything into a blender and give it a whirl! This dish tastes best chilled on a hot summer day with a generous swirl of tangy yogurt and (an optional) basil-jalapeño olive oil, but it's also an ideal make-ahead appetizer for a dinner party. Serve it up in shooters with a basil leaf for garnish. It's even better if some of the ingredients are fresh from your garden! Every spoonful is refreshing, tangy, slightly spicy, herby, and creamy—this gazpacho really has it all.

2 cups chopped mini cucumber, peeled or unpeeled
1 medium avocado, pit and skin removed
½ cup chopped yellow onion
½ cup chopped celery
¼ cup plain Greek yogurt
¼ cup olive oil
3 tbsp chopped basil
2 tbsp chopped jalapeño, seeds removed
2 tbsp chopped parsley
1½ tbsp white wine vinegar
1 large garlic clove
1¼ tsp kosher salt
1 tsp sugar or agave nectar
Olive oil or Basil Oil (page 254), to serve

1. In a blender, combine the cucumber, avocado, onion, celery, yogurt, oil, basil, jalapeño, parsley, white wine vinegar, garlic, salt, and agave and blend until completely smooth. For best results, cover and refrigerate the gazpacho for at least 1 hour (or overnight) before serving. Garnish with the oil before serving.

Make it plant-based: Use your favorite plant-based yogurt in place of the Greek yogurt.

Notes: If you prefer a thinner gazpacho, add up to an additional ¼ cup (60ml) water to the blender before blending and adjust salt as needed.

If you're sensitive to raw onion and garlic, dice both and rinse in a mesh colander under hot tap water for 30 seconds, then cold tap water for another 30 seconds to remove some of the bite.

SERVES 4-6 | PREP TIME: 10 MINUTES COOK TIME: 30 MINUTES

Roasted Cherry Tomato and Caprese Soup

with Burrata

This hearty yet summery dish is essentially a caprese salad in soup form. With two types of tomatoes (roasted cherry tomatoes and sun-dried), it's heavy on the rich tomato flavor, which is perfectly accented by a splash of balsamic vinegar. There's a bit of shredded mozzarella in the soup for flavor, but the star of the show is the rich, creamy dollop of fresh burrata on top. Fresh basil also makes an appearance twice, both in the soup and in a simple basil oil for topping, which you can skip if you're short on time. Finish it off with a few cracks of black pepper and some halved cherry tomatoes for a gorgeous summer appetizer or side.

FOR THE SOUP

- 3lb (1.35kg) cherry tomatoes
- 1 large yellow onion, roughly chopped
- 4 garlic cloves
- 3 tbsp olive oil
- 1½ tsp kosher salt, divided
- ½ tsp ground black pepper
- 2½ cups vegetable broth
- 1 cup shredded mozzarella cheese
- 2 tbsp oil-packed sun-dried tomatoes, drained and chopped
- 1½ tbsp balsamic vinegar
- ½ cup basil, loosely packed

FOR SERVING

- Extra-virgin olive oil or Basil Oil (page 254)
- 8oz (225g) burrata cheese, ripped into 4-6 even portions
- Basil, to garnish (optional)
- Cherry tomato halves, to garnish (optional)
- Black pepper, to garnish (optional)

1. Preheat the oven to 400°F (200°C).
2. To make the soup, on a sheet pan, toss together the cherry tomatoes, onion, garlic, olive oil, ¾ teaspoon of the salt, and pepper until well coated. Roast for 25 to 30 minutes, stirring halfway through, until the tomatoes are slightly blistered and have burst, releasing their juices.
3. About 10 minutes before the tomatoes are done cooking, in a small pot over medium heat, add the vegetable broth and heat until just steaming.
4. Once the tomato mixture is finished roasting, add it immediately to a blender. Make sure to scrape everything off the pan, including any accumulated juices. Add in the remaining ¾ teaspoon salt, the warmed broth, mozzarella, sun-dried tomatoes, balsamic vinegar, and basil. Blend for 1 minute, until completely smooth. If your blender has a small capacity, you may need to blend the soup in batches. Be sure to crack the lid slightly away from you as you blend to allow the steam to vent.
5. Divide the soup into 4 to 6 bowls, top each bowl with a portion of the burrata, and drizzle with the oil. Garnish with the basil, cherry tomatoes, and black pepper (if using). Serve immediately.

SERVES 6 | PREP TIME: 20 MINUTES COOK TIME: 1 HOUR AND 5 MINUTES

Roasted Poblano, Corn, and Potato Chowder

Corn chowder is a year-round comfort food. It works well in the summer when fresh corn is in season, served alongside grilled chicken, fish, or seared scallops. It's equally delicious in the winter months, when you can use frozen corn instead of fresh and serve it up with warm cornbread. This recipe requires a little bit of prep time to roast the poblanos, but it's worth the extra effort as it enhances their natural smokiness—however, they're not overly spicy, so this chowder has a gentle heat that pairs well with sweet corn. Serve it up with crumbled cotija cheese and a lime wedge.

2 poblano peppers
4 tbsp avocado or olive oil, divided
1 medium yellow onion, diced
3 garlic cloves, minced
3–4 large yellow potatoes, about 1lb (450g) in total, unpeeled and diced
2½ cups fresh or frozen sweet corn
1 cup diced celery
1½ tsp dried oregano
1½ tsp ground cumin
1½ tsp chili powder
1¼ tsp ground coriander
1¼ tsp kosher salt
½ cup whole milk
1½ tbsp gluten-free 1-to-1 flour (or regular all-purpose if not making it GF)
4 cups vegetable broth
2 tbsp chopped cilantro
2 tbsp freshly squeezed lime juice
Crumbled cotija cheese, to serve
Lime wedges, to serve

1. Position a rack at the top of the oven and preheat to 425°F (220°C). Line a small sheet pan with aluminum foil.
2. Place the poblano peppers on the sheet pan and roast on the top rack for 25 minutes, flipping the peppers every 5 to 10 minutes, until charred on all sides.
3. Using tongs, transfer the peppers to a medium bowl and cover tightly with plastic wrap. Let the peppers steam for about 15 minutes, then carefully peel off the skin. Remove the stem, then slice the peppers in half. Use a knife to scrape out the seeds and dice the peppers. Discard the stem and seeds.
4. To a large pot over medium heat, add 2 tablespoons of the oil. When the oil is hot and shimmers or slightly ripples, add in the onion and diced poblano peppers and cook for 5 minutes, stirring often, until the onion softens. Add in the garlic and cook for 2 additional minutes, stirring occasionally, until fragrant.
5. Add the remaining 2 tablespoons oil, then the potatoes, corn, celery, oregano, cumin, chili powder, coriander, and salt and continue cooking for 5 minutes, stirring occasionally, until the vegetables are slightly softened.
6. In a small bowl, whisk together the milk and flour until smooth. To the pot, add the flour mixture and the broth and stir well. Bring to a boil, then reduce the heat to low, cover with a lid, and cook for 25 minutes, stirring occasionally, until the potatoes are fork tender.
7. Stir in the cilantro and lime juice and remove from the heat. Serve hot with a garnish of cotija cheese and a lime wedge on the side.

Make it plant-based: Use full-fat oat milk in place of whole milk, and skip the cheese garnish.

SERVES 6 | **PREP TIME: 20 MINUTES** **COOK TIME: 50 MINUTES**

Fall Vegetable Minestrone

We love a bowl of brothy, vegetable-packed minestrone, but when fall vegetables are in season, we swap out zucchini and green beans for butternut squash and kale. This way, you get to enjoy fresh vegetables in a light, well-seasoned broth that serves as a welcome change-up from all of the heavy cream-based soups that are usually in the fall and winter rotation. The sausage is optional but turns this into a full, well-rounded meal.

1lb (450g) mild or spicy Italian sausage, casings removed
2 tbsp olive oil
1 medium yellow onion, diced
3 garlic cloves, minced
2 cups diced butternut or acorn squash, peeled and seeds removed
1 cup diced carrots
½ cup thinly sliced celery
2 tbsp tomato paste
1 tsp dried thyme
1 tsp dried oregano
1 tsp kosher salt
¼ tsp ground black pepper
6 cups vegetable or chicken broth
One 14½oz (411g) can diced tomatoes
⅔ cup ditalini or elbow pasta
One 15½oz (439g) can navy beans, drained and rinsed
2 cups chopped lacinato kale
¼ cup finely chopped parsley
¼ cup grated Parmesan, plus more to garnish
Red pepper flakes, to serve (optional)

1. In a large pot over medium heat, add the sausage and cook, breaking it up with a wooden spoon, for about 5 minutes, stirring regularly, until browned around the edges and mostly cooked through.
2. Add the oil and onion and cook for 5 minutes, stirring often, until the onions are softened and translucent. Add the garlic and cook for 1 more minute, until fragrant.
3. Stir in the squash, carrots, celery, tomato paste, thyme, oregano, salt, and pepper. Cook for 5 minutes, stirring often, until the vegetables start to soften.
4. Stir in the broth and diced tomatoes, then bring to a boil and reduce the heat to low. Cover with a lid and simmer for 25 minutes, stirring occasionally.
5. Meanwhile, bring a separate small pot of salted water to a boil. Cook the pasta according to package directions until al dente and drain.
6. Once the soup has simmered for 25 minutes, add the navy beans, kale, and parsley and continue cooking for about 3 minutes, until the kale is wilted. Just before serving, stir in the Parmesan and cooked pasta. (If preparing this dish ahead of time, keep the pasta separate from the soup, and combine just before serving.)
7. Serve hot with a garnish of grated Parmesan and red pepper flakes (if using).

Make it gluten-free: Swap in your favorite gluten-free pasta.

Make it plant-based: Leave out the sausage and cheese, or substitute with your favorite plant-based alternatives, and use vegetable broth.

SERVES 6 | PREP TIME: 15 MINUTES COOK TIME: 45 MINUTES

White Bean, Sausage, and Pumpkin Soup

If you're looking for a hearty, filling fall soup, stop here. With white beans, fresh pumpkin, spicy Italian chicken sausage, and sturdy greens, this soup is truly a full meal, especially served with some crusty bread. You likely won't be able to find fresh pie pumpkins in the US outside of the autumn months, but the good news is you can use any similar squash. We like butternut, acorn, or kabocha squashes, and sweet potatoes also work in a pinch!

- 4 tbsp olive oil, divided
- 1lb (450g) mild or spicy Italian chicken sausage, casings removed
- 1 medium yellow onion, diced
- 2 garlic cloves, minced
- 4 cups diced pumpkin or similar squash, peeled and seeds removed
- 1 cup thinly sliced celery
- 1 tbsp finely chopped thyme
- 1 tsp kosher salt
- ¼ tsp ground black pepper
- 8 cups chicken broth
- 3 cups destemmed, finely chopped curly kale
- One 15½oz (439g) can navy beans, drained and rinsed
- ¼ cup finely chopped parsley
- 2 tbsp freshly squeezed lemon juice
- Grated Parmesan, to serve (optional)
- Red pepper flakes, to serve (optional)

1. In a large pot over medium heat, add 3 tablespoons of the olive oil. When the oil is hot and shimmers or slightly ripples, add the sausage and cook for about 5 minutes, breaking it up with a wooden spoon, until browned around the edges and mostly cooked through.
2. Add the onion and cook for 4 to 5 minutes, stirring occasionally, until the onion is softened and translucent. Add the garlic and cook for 1 minute, until fragrant.
3. Add the remaining tablespoon olive oil, then stir in the pumpkin, celery, thyme, salt, and pepper and cook for 5 minutes, stirring occasionally, until the pumpkin and celery are softened.
4. Pour in the broth and increase the heat to high. Bring to a boil, then reduce the heat to low, cover with a lid, and simmer for 20 minutes, stirring occasionally, until the pumpkin is fork tender.
5. Stir in the kale, beans, parsley, and lemon juice, then simmer for 5 to 10 minutes, until the kale is wilted.
6. Serve topped with Parmesan and red pepper flakes (if using).

Make it vegetarian: Swap the sausage for more beans (or a plant-based sausage) and use vegetable broth instead of chicken broth.

STAUB
STAUB

SERVES 4 | **PREP TIME:** 15 MINUTES **COOK TIME:** 50 MINUTES

GF 

Coconut, Red Curry, and Lentil Soup

Creamy, spicy, flavorful, and packed with fiber and plant-based protein, this red lentil soup is a great addition to your soup repertoire. Fresh garlic, ginger, Thai red curry paste, and full-fat coconut milk make for a flavorful base for hearty vegetables like sweet potatoes and bell peppers. Blended until it's silky smooth, this soup is a good one for freezer meal prep since it's so easy to reheat. The curry roasted cashews add extra flavor and crunch. If you're plant-based, make sure to check the ingredients label for red curry paste before purchasing since some contain shrimp.

FOR THE CURRY-ROASTED CASHEWS

½ cup unsalted cashews
½ tbsp coconut oil, melted
1 tsp curry powder
¾ tsp light brown sugar or coconut sugar, packed
¼ tsp kosher salt
Pinch of cayenne pepper

FOR THE SOUP

3 tbsp coconut or avocado oil
1 medium yellow onion, diced
3 garlic cloves, minced
1 tbsp minced ginger
1 medium sweet potato, about 8oz (225g), peeled and diced
1 red bell pepper, diced
1 cup diced carrot
1½ tsp light brown sugar or coconut sugar, packed
1 tsp kosher salt, plus more to taste
1 tsp ground cumin
¼ tsp cayenne pepper
3–4 tbsp Thai red curry paste (without shrimp), to taste
2 tbsp tomato paste
4 cups vegetable broth
One 13½oz (400ml) can full-fat coconut milk
¾ cup red lentils, rinsed
¼ cup finely chopped cilantro
3 tbsp freshly squeezed lime juice

1. Preheat the oven to 300°F (150°C). Line a sheet pan with parchment paper.
2. To make the curry-roasted cashews, in a medium bowl, stir together the cashews, melted coconut oil, curry powder, brown sugar, salt, and cayenne pepper until evenly coated. Transfer to the sheet pan and bake for 13 to 15 minutes, stirring halfway through, until the cashews look mostly dry. Remove from the oven and set aside to cool in the pan.
3. To make the soup, to a large pot over medium heat, add the oil. When the oil is hot and shimmers or slightly ripples, add the onions and cook for 3 minutes, stirring occasionally, until they start to soften. Stir in the garlic and ginger and cook for 2 minutes, stirring often, until fragrant.
4. Stir in the sweet potato, bell pepper, carrot, sugar, salt, cumin, and cayenne pepper and cook for 5 minutes, stirring occasionally, until the carrots are slightly softened.
5. Add the red curry paste and tomato paste and stir well to coat, then add the vegetable broth, coconut milk, lentils, and cilantro. Bring to a boil, then reduce the heat to low, cover with a lid, and cook for about 25 minutes, stirring occasionally, until the vegetables are fork tender.
6. Carefully transfer the soup to a blender, filling it only halfway and working in batches as needed. Add the lime juice and blend until smooth, making sure to crack the lid of the blender slightly facing away from you to let steam escape. Taste and add more salt if desired. Serve immediately, topped with the curry-roasted cashews.

SERVES 4–6 | PREP TIME: 15 MINUTES COOK TIME: 40 MINUTES

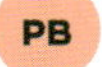

Creamy Lemon Rice Soup

This is the soup recipe we make most often, and it never gets old! It's rich and creamy thanks to a secret ingredient: blended white beans. Whether you're feeling under the weather or just need a cozy, nourishing meal on a cold winter night, this soup is there when you need it most. To make it extra filling, we sometimes add shredded rotisserie chicken before serving. Keep in mind that the rice soaks up a lot of liquid, so if you have leftovers, you'll need to stir in more broth when reheating.

3 tbsp olive oil
1 small yellow onion, diced
1½ cups diced carrots
1 cup diced celery
3 garlic cloves, minced
One 15½oz (439g) can cannellini beans, drained and rinsed
6 cups vegetable broth, divided
½ cup arborio rice
3 bay leaves
2 tsp kosher salt
1 tsp dried oregano
½ tsp ground black pepper
2 cups baby spinach, packed
¼ cup freshly squeezed lemon juice, plus more to taste
¼ cup finely chopped parsley
2 tbsp finely chopped dill

1. To a large pot over medium heat, add the olive oil. When the oil is hot and shimmers or slightly ripples, add the onion and cook for 5 to 7 minutes, stirring often, until translucent.
2. Stir in the carrots, celery, and garlic and cook for another 5 to 7 minutes, stirring occasionally, until the carrots and celery are softened.
3. To a blender, add the beans and 1 cup of the vegetable broth and blend until smooth. Transfer the blended beans to the soup pot and add the remaining 5 cups vegetable broth, as well as the rice, bay leaves, salt, oregano, and pepper. Bring the soup to a boil, then reduce the heat to low, cover with a lid, and simmer for about 25 minutes, stirring occasionally so the rice doesn't stick to the bottom of the pot, until the rice is al dente.
4. Stir in the spinach, lemon juice, parsley, and dill and cook for 5 minutes, until the spinach is wilted. Taste and add more of the lemon juice as desired. Remove the bay leaves, then serve hot.

SERVES 6 | **PREP TIME:** 20 MINUTES **COOK TIME:** 45 MINUTES

Creamy Chicken and Mushroom Wild Rice Soup

Umami-rich mushrooms, nutty wild rice, and chicken team up to make a nourishing, comforting meal that isn't overly heavy. We like to use a few different types of mushrooms for maximum flavor, especially shiitake and cremini, but button and other wild mushrooms work great too. If you can find a package of mixed wild mushrooms at the grocery store, this is the perfect way to use them. A splash of sherry adds depth of flavor, but if you don't have any, white wine is a great substitute.

¼ cup olive oil
1 cup diced yellow onion
3 garlic cloves, minced
1lb (450g) mushrooms, thinly sliced
1 cup thinly sliced carrots
1 cup thinly sliced celery
1 tbsp finely chopped thyme
2 tsp finely chopped rosemary
1 tsp kosher salt
¾ tsp sweet paprika
¼ tsp ground black pepper
⅓ cup dry sherry
6 cups vegetable broth, divided
3 tbsp all-purpose flour
2 bay leaves
½ cup wild rice blend, cooked according to package instructions, warm
8oz (225g) shredded rotisserie chicken
½ cup half-and-half or heavy cream
1 tbsp freshly squeezed lemon juice

1. To a large pot over medium heat, add the olive oil. When the oil is hot and shimmers or slightly ripples, add the onion and cook for about 5 minutes, stirring occasionally, until soft and translucent. Add in the garlic and cook for another 1 to 2 minutes, until fragrant.
2. Stir in the mushrooms, carrots, celery, thyme, rosemary, salt, paprika, and pepper. Cook, stirring often, for 6 to 8 minutes, until the mushrooms have released most of their moisture.
3. Add in the sherry and let simmer for 1 to 2 minutes, until the alcohol cooks off, scraping the pan with a spatula or wooden spoon to remove any caramelized bits stuck to the bottom.
4. In a small bowl, whisk together 1 cup of the vegetable broth with the flour until no clumps remain. To the soup pot, add the broth-flour mixture and the remaining 5 cups vegetable broth. Bring to a boil, then reduce the heat to low and simmer for about 25 minutes, until the soup is thickened and the carrots are nearly fork tender.
5. Stir in the cooked wild rice, chicken, half-and-half, and lemon juice, then cook over low heat for 10 to 15 minutes, until the chicken is warmed through and the carrots are completely fork tender. Serve right away.

Make it gluten-free: Use gluten-free 1-to-1 or measure-for-measure flour.

Make it plant-based: Add an extra 8 ounces (225g) mixed mushrooms in place of the chicken and use plant-based cream instead of half-and-half.

SERVES 6 | PREP TIME: 20 MINUTES COOK TIME: 30 MINUTES

Turmeric-Ginger Chicken and Orzo Soup

Also known as "sick-day soup" in our house, this dish is packed with nourishing, immune-boosting ingredients like garlic, ginger, turmeric, red bell pepper, lemon, and leafy greens. If you really are under the weather, you'll want to keep prep as easy as possible, which is why we use shredded rotisserie chicken. If you'd rather make it yourself, add two or three boneless, skinless chicken breasts to the soup once you add in the broth. Once the chicken is cooked through, use two forks to shred it. Keep in mind that the orzo will absorb a lot of liquid overnight in the fridge, so you may need to add in more broth when reheating.

- 3 tbsp olive oil
- 1½ cups diced yellow onion
- 3 garlic cloves, minced
- 1 tbsp minced turmeric, peeled, or 1 tsp ground turmeric
- 1 tbsp minced ginger, peeled
- 1 cup thinly sliced celery
- 1 cup diced red bell pepper
- 1 cup sliced carrots
- 1 tsp kosher salt
- ½ tsp ground black pepper
- 8 cups chicken or vegetable broth
- 2 cups shredded rotisserie chicken
- ½ cup orzo
- 4 cups chopped lacinato kale, destemmed
- ¼ cup chopped parsley
- 2 tbsp freshly squeezed lemon juice

1. To a large pot over medium heat, add the olive oil. Once the oil is hot and shimmers or ripples slightly, stir in the onion, garlic, turmeric, and ginger and cook for 5 minutes, stirring often, until the onion is softened and fragrant.
2. Use a slotted spoon to remove the onion, garlic, turmeric, and ginger from the skillet and transfer to a blender with the broth. Blend for about 30 seconds, until smooth.
3. To the same skillet, add the celery, bell pepper, carrots, salt, and pepper and cook for another 5 minutes, stirring occasionally, until the vegetables start to soften.
4. Stir in the broth mixture, increase the heat to high, and bring to a boil. Stir in the chicken and orzo. Reduce the heat to low, cover with a lid, and simmer for about 10 minutes, until the orzo has begun to soften.
5. Stir in the kale, parsley, and lemon juice and cook for 5 to 10 minutes, until the kale is wilted and the orzo is al dente. Serve hot.

Make it gluten-free: Use a small gluten-free pasta of choice.

Make it plant-based: Replace the chicken with a 15½ ounces (439g) can of rinsed chickpeas or white beans, and use vegetable broth instead of chicken broth.

Salads

SERVES 4–5 | PREP TIME: 25 MINUTES COOK TIME: 20 MINUTES

V

Roasted Radish Salad
with Green Goddess Dressing

Roasting a radish *completely* changes its flavor profile from peppery and sharp to mild, slightly sweet, and pleasantly earthy—somewhat similar to a turnip. In fact, you might have a hard time believing it's the same vegetable you started with! It's the perfect spring vegetable to pair with crisp, fresh peas, tender butter lettuce, and a super creamy yogurt-based, herb-packed green goddess dressing.

FOR THE RADISHES

1½ cups trimmed, quartered radishes
2 tsp olive oil
1 tsp honey
¼ tsp kosher salt
Ground black pepper, to taste

FOR THE GREEN GODDESS DRESSING

¼ cup plain yogurt
¼ cup mayonnaise
¼ cup chopped herbs of choice (basil, chives, tarragon, parsley, cilantro, etc.)
1 tbsp freshly squeezed lemon juice
1 small garlic clove, minced
1 tsp capers, drained
¼ tsp kosher salt
⅛ tsp ground black pepper

FOR THE SALAD

2 medium heads of butter lettuce, about 9oz (250g) in total, chopped
1 cup sliced baby cucumber
½ cup snap peas, sliced thinly on a bias
¼ cup roasted salted sunflower seeds
2 tbsp chopped chives

1. Preheat the oven to 400°F (200°C).
2. To make the radishes, in a medium bowl, toss the radishes, olive oil, honey, salt, and pepper to evenly coat. Transfer to a sheet pan and roast for 15 to 20 minutes, stirring once halfway through, until the radishes are fork tender and slightly caramelized around the edges. Remove from the oven and set aside to cool in the sheet pan.
3. To make the dressing, in a small blender or food processor, combine the yogurt, mayonnaise, herbs, lemon juice, garlic, capers, salt, pepper, and 1 tablespoon water and blend until smooth.
4. To make the salad, to a large bowl or platter, add the lettuce. Drizzle with half the dressing and toss to coat. Top the salad with the roasted radishes, cucumber, snap peas, sunflower seeds, and chives. Finish with more dressing to taste and toss lightly before serving.

Make it plant-based: Use agave instead of honey, and use your favorite plant-based yogurt and mayo.

SERVES 4 | PREP TIME: 20 MINUTES

Berry, Avocado, and Spinach Salad

Crisp, vibrant, and bursting with flavor, this salad is a celebration of fresh summer ingredients. Baby spinach is the perfect leafy base for the sweet, juicy berries, while avocado and goat cheese add creaminess, cucumber adds freshness, and roasted pepitas add some crunch. A zesty jalapeño-lime vinaigrette ties it all together, delivering just the right amount of heat to balance the sweetness. If you're not a fan of spinach, arugula works just as well. Pair this salad with our Turkey Burgers with Blueberry Compote and Jalapeño-Basil Aioli (page 138) and Perfect Herb-Roasted Potatoes (page 167) for a delicious summer dinner.

FOR THE JALAPEÑO-LIME DRESSING

⅓ cup avocado or olive oil
2 tbsp minced jalapeño, seeds removed
2 tbsp freshly squeezed lime juice
1½ tbsp finely chopped mint
½ tbsp honey
1 tsp lime zest
¾ tsp kosher salt

FOR THE SALAD

5oz (140g) baby spinach
1½ cups berries of choice (blueberries, blackberries, raspberries, strawberries, etc.)
1 cup thinly sliced baby cucumber
1 avocado, diced or thinly sliced
½ cup crumbled goat cheese
⅓ cup roasted salted pepitas (optional)

1. To make the dressing, in a small bowl, whisk together the oil, jalapeño, lime juice, mint, honey, lime zest, and salt. Set aside.
2. To make the salad, to a small bowl, add the spinach and pour half the dressing over top. Toss to coat. Add the berries, cucumber, avocado, goat cheese, pepitas (if using), and more dressing to taste. Toss gently to combine, then serve right away.

Make it plant-based: Use agave instead of honey, and leave out the goat cheese or use your favorite plant-based soft cheese alternative.

SERVES 4–6 | **PREP TIME: 20 MINUTES**

Michigan Cherry Salad

V

If you go to any local Michigan restaurant, you're likely to find some variation of this salad on the menu. Michigan is known for its cherries—believe it or not, there are entire stores dedicated to cherry-themed products. This salad combines super tart dried cherries with a flavorful cherry vinaigrette. (You can use fresh or frozen cherries, depending on availability.) Candied pecans or walnuts are a must, and you can change up the cheese based on your preference. Try feta, gorgonzola, or cubed halloumi.

FOR THE CHERRY VINAIGRETTE

8 fresh or frozen sweet cherries, pitted (see note)
2 tbsp olive oil
1 tbsp apple cider vinegar
½ tbsp balsamic vinegar
½ tbsp maple syrup
½ tsp Dijon mustard
¼ tsp kosher salt
⅛ tsp ground black pepper

FOR THE SALAD

5oz (140g) mixed spring greens
¾ cup diced Honeycrisp apple
½ cup toasted pecans or Quick Candied Nuts (page 258)
½ cup dried tart cherries, or 1 cup halved fresh cherries
½ cup crumbled goat cheese

1. To make the vinaigrette, to a small blender or food processor, add the cherries, olive oil, apple cider vinegar, balsamic vinegar, maple syrup, Dijon mustard, salt, and pepper. Blend until smooth.
2. To make the salad, in a large bowl, combine the spring greens and half the dressing. Toss to evenly coat.
3. Add the apple, nuts, dried cherries, and goat cheese, then drizzle with more dressing to taste and serve.

Make it plant-based: Leave out the goat cheese, or use your favorite plant-based soft cheese alternative.

Note: If using frozen cherries, thaw before blending them to make the vinaigrette.

SERVES 6–8 | PREP TIME: 20 MINUTES

Mango Cabbage Slaw

Lexi: My husband and I can never turn down an opportunity to use fresh mango. You may not think to add it to a slaw, but it's the star ingredient here. With carrots, snow peas, edamame, and two types of cabbage—mango is the sweet, tart, and juicy component that balances out all the crunchy ingredients, and the spicy ginger-lime dressing really brightens everything up. This is a salad you can enjoy on its own or use as a topping for grilled fish.

FOR THE SLAW

3 cups thinly sliced Napa cabbage
1½ cups thinly sliced red cabbage
1 cup julienned carrots (see notes)
1 cup thinly sliced snow peas
1 cup frozen shelled edamame, cooked according to package directions and cooled
1 cup thinly sliced mango
½ cup roasted peanuts
⅓ cup finely chopped green onions
2 tbsp finely chopped cilantro

FOR THE SPICY GINGER-LIME DRESSING

¼ cup sesame oil
2 tbsp freshly squeezed lime juice
2 tbsp soy sauce
1 tbsp rice wine vinegar
1 tbsp sriracha
½ tbsp agave
1 tbsp minced ginger
1½ garlic cloves, minced
1 tsp lime zest

1. To make the slaw, in a large bowl, combine the Napa cabbage, red cabbage, carrots, snow peas, edamame, mango, peanuts, green onions, and cilantro. Set aside.
2. To make the dressing, in a medium bowl, whisk together the sesame oil, lime juice, soy sauce, rice wine vinegar, sriracha, agave, ginger, garlic, and lime zest.
3. Pour the dressing over the slaw and toss until well combined. Serve right away, or refrigerate for up to 1 hour before serving.

Notes: To julienne a carrot, begin by cutting the carrot into two or three sections about 2 to 3 inches (5 to 7.5cm) long. You'll only be able to julienne the thicker portions of the carrot. Slice each chunk lengthwise into thin planks. Stack a few planks on top of each other and slice them lengthwise into thin matchstick-size strips.

For extra-crunchy slaw that doesn't get too soggy as it sits, salt your cabbage before combining with the rest of the ingredients. To do so, place the sliced cabbage in a colander, sprinkle with 1 teaspoon kosher salt, and use your hands to toss. Let sit for 1 hour, then rinse the cabbage and use a salad spinner to remove as much moisture as possible.

SERVES 4 | **PREP TIME:** 15 MINUTES **COOK TIME:** 10 MINUTES

V

Peach, Tomato, and Burrata Salad
with Crispy Breadcrumbs

Think of this salad as a caprese, but extra fancy. Fresh, juicy summer peaches pair perfectly with ripe tomatoes, creamy burrata (or mozzarella, if that's easier to find), fresh basil, crisp and buttery breadcrumbs for a bit of crunch, and a tangy champagne vinaigrette. It's the ideal hot weather appetizer when you don't want to turn on the oven, or when you really want to load up on peak summer flavors. Pair this with our Citrus-Herb Chicken Kebabs (page 131) or Hot Honey Panko Chicken Cutlets (page 145) and your favorite grain for a full meal.

FOR THE BREADCRUMBS

2 tbsp unsalted butter
½ cup panko breadcrumbs
¼ tsp dried basil
⅛ tsp garlic powder
Kosher salt and ground black pepper, to taste

FOR THE CHAMPAGNE VINAIGRETTE

¼ cup olive oil
2 tbsp champagne vinegar
2 tsp Dijon mustard
1 tsp honey
¼ tsp kosher salt
⅛ tsp ground black pepper

FOR THE SALAD

3 cups halved cherry tomatoes, or 2–3 large heirloom tomatoes, thinly sliced
2 medium peaches, thinly sliced
8oz (225g) burrata cheese, torn into ½–1oz (15–30g) portions
Basil, to garnish

1. To make the breadcrumbs, in a medium skillet over medium heat, melt the butter. Once the butter is bubbling, add the breadcrumbs, basil, garlic powder, and salt and pepper to taste. Stir to evenly coat the breadcrumbs in the oil and spices.
2. Spread the breadcrumbs into an even layer and cook for 1 to 2 minutes, until they start to brown. Stir, then cook for another 1 to 2 minutes, until the breadcrumbs are golden brown. Transfer to a bowl and set aside to cool.
3. To make the vinaigrette, in a small bowl, whisk the olive oil, champagne vinegar, Dijon mustard, honey, salt, and pepper until emulsified.
4. To make the salad, on a serving platter, arrange the tomatoes, peaches, and burrata. Drizzle the vinaigrette over top to taste, then sprinkle with the toasted breadcrumbs. Garnish with fresh basil before serving.

Make it gluten-free: Use gluten-free breadcrumbs.

SERVES 6 | **PREP TIME:** 15 MINUTES, PLUS MARINATING TIME **COOK TIME:** 35 MINUTES

Grilled Shrimp Salad

with Old Bay Croutons and Creamy Lemon-Chive Dressing

This is the type of salad that's truly a full meal. There's a little bit of everything: marinated grilled shrimp for protein, plenty of fresh vegetables, crispy seasoned croutons for carbs, plus a creamy lemon-chive dressing. If you don't want to fire up the grill for the shrimp, use a grill pan or sauté them instead. The Old Bay croutons are our favorite part, and we usually make extra just for snacking. If you don't have any Old Bay, Cajun seasoning can be a good (and slightly spicier) alternative.

FOR THE OLD BAY CROUTONS

- 6oz (175g) sourdough or Italian bread, cut into 1-inch (2.5cm) cubes
- ¼ cup olive oil
- 1 tbsp Old Bay seasoning

FOR THE SHRIMP

- ⅓ cup olive or avocado oil
- 3 tbsp freshly squeezed lemon juice
- 1½ tsp sweet paprika
- 1 tsp kosher salt
- ¾ tsp garlic powder
- ½ tsp ground black pepper
- ⅛ tsp cayenne pepper
- 26–30 raw shrimp, about 2lb (900g) in total; shells, veins, and tails removed
- Wooden skewers, 6–8 inches (15–20cm) long

FOR THE SALAD

- 1½ cups fresh or frozen corn kernels
- 8 cups chopped romaine lettuce
- 12oz (350g) cherry tomatoes, halved
- 1 large avocado, diced or thinly sliced
- ½ small red onion, thinly sliced

FOR THE LEMON-CHIVE DRESSING

- ¼ cup olive or avocado oil
- 2 tbsp mayonnaise
- 2 tbsp finely chopped chives, plus more to garnish
- 1½ tbsp freshly squeezed lemon juice
- ½ tsp lemon zest
- ½ tsp agave nectar or granulated sugar
- ½ tsp kosher salt
- ¼ tsp ground black pepper
- ¼ tsp garlic powder
- ¼ tsp onion powder
- ½ tsp sweet paprika

1. Preheat the oven to 375°F (190°C).
2. To make the croutons, in a large bowl, combine the bread, olive oil, and Old Bay seasoning. Using your hands, toss the bread until it's well coated, then transfer to a sheet pan and spread into an even layer. Bake for 17 to 20 minutes, stirring halfway through, until the bread is golden brown. Set aside to cool in the sheet pan.
3. To make the shrimp, in a large bowl, whisk together the oil, lemon juice, paprika, salt, garlic powder, black pepper, and cayenne pepper. Add the shrimp and stir to coat. Let marinate for 15 to 20 minutes.
4. Heat a grill pan or a grill to medium-high heat. Thread the shrimp onto the wooden skewers, reserving about 2 tablespoons of the marinade. Place in the hot grill pan and cook for 2 to 3 minutes per side, until the shrimp is slightly charred and opaque. Remove from the heat and set aside on a platter to cool.

5. To make the salad, in a medium skillet over medium heat, add the reserved 2 tablespoons marinade. Once bubbling, add the corn. Cook for 6 to 8 minutes, stirring often, until the kernels are softened, then remove from the heat and let cool.
6. To a large salad bowl, add the lettuce, cherry tomatoes, avocado, onion, croutons, shrimp, and corn. Set aside.
7. To make the dressing, in a medium bowl, whisk together the oil, mayonnaise, chives, lemon juice, lemon zest, agave, salt, pepper, garlic powder, onion powder, and paprika until emulsified.
8. Drizzle the dressing over the salad. Toss lightly before serving.

SERVES 6–8 | **PREP TIME:** 20 MINUTES **COOK TIME:** 10 MINUTES

Sun-Dried Tomato and Orzo Salad

V

Since there's no lettuce in this dish, our pasta salad doesn't get soggy, so it's a meal-prep mainstay for us. Plus, it tastes even better the next day. Artichokes, sun-dried tomatoes, and kalamata olives pack a big punch of Mediterranean flavor. You might be used to pasta salads that congeal in the fridge, but this is not one of those. Because orzo is so small, it doesn't dry out, and it stays moist without getting mushy. If you want to make this into a full meal, serve it alongside our Citrus-Herb Chicken Kebabs (page 131).

FOR THE ORZO AND PINE NUTS

8oz (225g) orzo pasta
⅓ cup pine nuts

FOR THE DRESSING

¼ cup olive oil
2 tbsp freshly squeezed lemon juice
2 tsp Dijon mustard
½ tbsp red wine vinegar
¾ tsp kosher salt
½ tsp garlic powder
¼ tsp ground black pepper
¼ tsp red pepper flakes

FOR THE SALAD

2 cups chopped baby spinach
½ cup marinated artichoke hearts, drained and chopped
½ cup kalamata olives, drained and quartered
½ cup oil-packed sun-dried tomatoes, drained and chopped
½ cup shredded Parmesan
⅓ cup finely diced red onion
1 tbsp finely chopped parsley
¼ cup finely chopped basil

1. In a medium pot filled with salted water, cook the orzo al dente according to package instructions. Drain and set aside to cool.
2. Meanwhile, make the pine nuts by toasting in a small skillet over medium-low heat for about 5 minutes, stirring frequently, until lightly browned and fragrant. Transfer to a plate and set aside.
3. To make the dressing, in a medium bowl, whisk together the olive oil, lemon juice, Dijon mustard, red wine vinegar, salt, garlic powder, black pepper, and red pepper flakes until emulsified.
4. To make the salad, in a large bowl, combine the cooked orzo, spinach, artichokes, olives, sun-dried tomatoes, Parmesan, onion, parsley, and basil. Stir well to combine. Drizzle the dressing over top and toss until well coated.
5. Garnish with the toasted pine nuts right before serving.

Make it gluten-free: Use your favorite gluten-free orzo or another small gluten-free pasta of choice.

Make it plant-based: Leave out the Parmesan or substitute it with your favorite plant-based alternative.

SERVES 4–5 | **PREP TIME: 20 MINUTES**

Greek Chickpea Salad

Lexi: There's no recipe in this book I have made more than this chickpea salad. It's as refreshing, crunchy, and tangy as it is colorful and easy to make. If I'm being honest, I usually just eyeball the ingredients, because any combination of them will end up tasting good. The dressing is my favorite part—it's super tangy and bright, and it also doubles as an easy marinade for chicken or fish. The dressing will pool on the bottom of the bowl as it sits, so give it a good stir before serving. I like to whip up a batch when we order a pizza. It's much better than a basic pizzeria salad, and it's the perfect complement to a greasy slice.

FOR THE GREEK VINAIGRETTE

¼ cup olive oil
3 tbsp red wine vinegar
1 tbsp freshly squeezed lemon juice
1 tsp Dijon mustard
¾ tsp dried oregano
½ tsp garlic powder
¼ tsp kosher salt
¼ tsp ground black pepper

FOR THE SALAD

One 15½oz (439g) can chickpeas, drained and rinsed
1½ cups diced mini cucumber
1½ cups quartered cherry tomatoes
1 large red or yellow bell pepper, diced
½ cup kalamata olives, drained and quartered
3oz (85g) crumbled feta cheese

1. To make the vinaigrette, in a small bowl, whisk together the olive oil, vinegar, lemon juice, Dijon mustard, oregano, garlic powder, salt, and black pepper.
2. To make the salad, in a large bowl, combine the chickpeas, cucumber, cherry tomatoes, bell pepper, olives, and feta. Pour the dressing over top and toss well to combine.

Make it plant-based: Leave out the feta cheese or substitute it with your favorite plant-based alternative.

SERVES 6 | **PREP TIME: 25 MINUTES** **COOK TIME: 40 MINUTES**

White Bean Niçoise Salad
with Roasted Potatoes

If we could bottle and sell one salad dressing from this cookbook (or our website in general), it would absolutely be this vinaigrette. It's so tangy and umami-rich thanks to a small amount of soy sauce and miso, which really elevates a simple salad to something special. A Niçoise is traditionally made with tuna, but to keep this recipe vegetarian, we use white beans instead. The roasted potatoes are unbelievably delicious on their own, and they really round out this salad into a full meal. The cherry on top? Crispy fried capers. You can skip this step if you don't have the time, but we think it's worth the effort.

FOR THE POTATOES

3 tbsp olive oil
1 tbsp Dijon mustard
1½ tsp herbes de Provence or Italian seasoning blend
½ tsp kosher salt
¼ tsp ground black pepper
¼ tsp garlic powder
1lb (450g) mini yellow potatoes, halved

FOR THE CAPERS

Vegetable oil
3 tbsp capers, drained and patted dry

FOR THE VINAIGRETTE

⅓ cup olive oil
2 tbsp champagne or white wine vinegar
2 tbsp minced shallots
2 tsp soy sauce
2 tsp mild white or yellow miso
1 tsp Dijon mustard
½ tsp herbes de Provence or Italian seasoning blend
¼ tsp garlic powder
Ground black pepper, to taste

FOR THE SALAD

1 tsp kosher salt
6oz (175g) thin French green beans, trimmed
One 15½oz (439g) can white beans, drained and rinsed
1 large head of romaine lettuce, about 10oz (285g), chopped
1 cup (225g) halved cherry tomatoes
⅓ cup kalamata olives, drained and quartered
4 hard-boiled eggs, halved

1. Preheat the oven to 375°F (190°C).
2. To make the potatoes, in a medium bowl, whisk together the olive oil, Dijon mustard, herbes de Provence, salt, pepper, and garlic powder until well combined. Add the potatoes and toss until evenly coated.
3. Transfer the potatoes to a sheet pan and roast for 35 to 40 minutes, stirring once or twice halfway through, until crispy and fork tender. Remove from the oven and set aside on the sheet pan to cool.
4. To make the capers, to a small pot over medium heat, add about ¼ inch (5mm) of the vegetable oil. While the oil heats, line a plate with a paper towel. When the oil reaches 350°F (180°C), add the capers and cook for 2 to 3 minutes, stirring often, until crispy. Transfer to the lined plate to cool, letting the paper towel soak up excess oil. Set aside.
5. To make the vinaigrette, in a small bowl or measuring cup, whisk the olive oil, vinegar, shallots, soy sauce, miso, Dijon mustard, herbes de

Provence, garlic powder, and ground black pepper until emulsified. Set aside.

6. To make the salad, to a medium pot over high heat, add 1 quart of water and the kosher salt and bring to a boil. Meanwhile, prepare a large bowl with ice water. To the boiling water, add the green beans, then reduce the heat to medium and simmer for about 3 minutes, until the green beans are just slightly tender. With a slotted spoon, immediately transfer the green beans to the bowl with ice water. Let sit for 5 minutes, then drain the green beans and set aside to dry. (Tip: You can reuse this hot water for hard-boiling the eggs, if you need to make them at this stage.)
7. In a medium bowl, combine the white beans and 2 to 3 tablespoons of the vinaigrette. Stir to coat and let sit while preparing the remaining ingredients.
8. In a large salad bowl or on a platter, spread out the lettuce. Top the salad with the roasted potatoes, green beans, white beans, tomatoes, olives, hard-boiled eggs, and capers. Drizzle the dressing over top and serve.

Make it plant-based: Leave out the eggs or substitute them with additional white beans to taste.

SERVES 6 | **PREP TIME:** 15 MINUTES **COOK TIME:** 20 MINUTES

Fall Cobb Salad

GF

Lexi: Yes, it is exactly what it sounds like: a Cobb salad, but with fall ingredients. And honestly, this is kind of the only way I want to eat Cobb salad from now on! We keep some of the classic components, like hard-boiled eggs, crispy bacon, grilled chicken, and romaine, but add autumnal roasted squash, apple, and cranberries. We also swap out blue cheese for crumbled goat cheese and add a simple maple-mustard dressing. This is far from a boring salad, and it will have you looking forward to lunch!

FOR THE SQUASH

8oz (225g) acorn or butternut squash, peeled, seeds removed, and diced
1 tbsp olive oil
Kosher salt and ground black pepper, to taste

FOR THE DRESSING

3 tbsp olive oil
2 tbsp apple cider vinegar
1 tbsp Dijon mustard
1 tbsp mayonnaise
1 tsp maple syrup
½ tsp kosher salt
¼ tsp ground black pepper
¼ tsp garlic powder
¼ tsp onion powder

FOR THE SALAD

8 cups chopped romaine lettuce
6 slices of cooked thick-cut bacon, 6oz (175g) in total, crumbled
4 large hard-boiled eggs, chopped
1 medium Honeycrisp apple, diced
½ cup diced celery
½ cup crumbled goat cheese
⅓ cup dried cranberries
6–8oz (175–225g) cooked chicken breast, diced (optional)

1. To make the squash, preheat the oven to 375°F (190°C). Line a small sheet pan with parchment paper.
2. In a medium bowl, combine the squash and olive oil and season with salt and pepper to taste. Toss until well coated. Transfer the squash to the sheet pan and roast for 20 minutes, flipping the pieces halfway through, until fork tender and browned around the edges. Set aside.
3. To make the dressing, in a small bowl, whisk together the olive oil, apple cider vinegar, Dijon mustard, mayonnaise, maple syrup, salt, black pepper, garlic powder and onion powder until emulsified.
4. To make the salad, to a large salad bowl, add the lettuce and half of the dressing and toss to coat. Add the roasted butternut squash, bacon, eggs, apple, celery, goat cheese, cranberries, and chicken (if using). Drizzle more dressing over the salad and serve immediately.

SERVES 6 | PREP TIME: 20 MINUTES COOK TIME: 30 MINUTES

Shaved Brussels Sprout Salad

This has been the most popular holiday recipe on our website for 2 years in a row, so we absolutely had to include the fan favorite in our book. Raw brussels sprouts might not sound appealing, but when they're thinly shaved, they make for the perfect crunchy slaw-like salad base. They hold onto the creamy Dijon vinaigrette well without getting soggy—you can even make the salad a day in advance. We like to add in our winter favorites, like tart dried cranberries, crisp diced apple, and pomegranate arils for a pop of sweetness. The star of the show, however, is the crunchy, salty sweet, and nutty pepita brittle. You're going to want to make a double batch because it's also delicious as a snack. If you don't want to make the brittle, you can instead use ¾ cup roasted pepitas. Add this dish to your next fall or winter menu—we promise it will disappear quickly!

FOR THE PEPITA BRITTLE

¾ cup raw unsalted pepitas
2 tbsp maple syrup
1½ tsp finely chopped thyme
1 tsp olive oil
½ tsp kosher salt
¼ tsp ground black pepper

FOR THE SALAD

1lb (450g) brussels sprouts, trimmed and shredded (see note)
1½ cups thinly sliced lacinato kale, destemmed
1 cup diced Honeycrisp apple
⅔ cup dried cranberries
¾ cup pomegranate arils, divided
1½oz (45g) Manchego cheese, thinly shaved or grated

FOR THE DRESSING

¼ cup olive oil
2 tbsp freshly squeezed lemon juice
2 tbsp apple cider vinegar
2 tbsp Dijon mustard
1½ tbsp maple syrup
1 tsp kosher salt
½ tsp ground black pepper

1. Preheat the oven to 275°F (140°C). Line a small sheet pan with parchment paper.
2. To make the pepita brittle, in a small bowl, stir together the pepitas, maple syrup, thyme, olive oil, salt, and pepper until well coated. Spread the mixture evenly on the prepared sheet pan in a thin layer. Bake for about 30 minutes, rotating the pan halfway through. The seeds should be lightly browned but not burned. Let cool to room temperature on the pan before breaking into pieces, then set aside.
3. To make the salad, in a large bowl, combine the brussels sprouts, kale, apple, dried cranberries, and ½ cup of the pomegranate arils. Set aside.
4. To make the dressing, in a small bowl, whisk together the olive oil, lemon juice, apple cider vinegar, Dijon mustard, maple syrup, salt, and pepper until emulsified. Pour the dressing over the salad to taste and toss well to coat.
5. Before serving, top the salad with the pepita brittle, the remaining ¼ cup pomegranate arils, and the Manchego cheese.

Make it plant-based: Leave out the cheese or substitute it with your favorite plant-based alternative.

Note: To shred the brussels sprouts as thinly as possible, use a food processor with a slicing disc set to $\frac{1}{16}$ inch (1.5mm) thick or use a mandoline (with extra care) or a knife.

SERVES 4 | **PREP TIME:** 20 MINUTES **COOK TIME:** 15 MINUTES

Halloumi, Couscous, and Pomegranate Salad

with Za'atar Vinaigrette

If you've never had halloumi, I'm sorry to say that you've been missing out. The semihard cheese from Cyprus is made of goat and sheep milk and has a high melting point, which means it can be grilled or fried but retain its shape, making it the perfect addition to a salad. It's almost like cheese croutons! Can't go wrong with that. It's salty and tangy and develops a perfect crispy crust that we simply can't get enough of. This is best paired with Mediterranean-inspired ingredients, like couscous (we use large pearl couscous), pomegranate, pickled onion, pistachios, fresh oranges for a pop of sweetness, and a tangy za'atar-spiced vinaigrette that also works as a great marinade for tofu, chicken, shrimp, or beef.

FOR THE COUSCOUS AND HALOUMI

- ½ cup pearl couscous
- Kosher salt, to taste
- 8oz (225g) halloumi cheese, cut into 1 x ¼-inch (2.5cm x 6mm) slices

FOR THE ZA'ATAR VINAIGRETTE

- ⅓ cup olive oil
- 2 tbsp freshly squeezed lemon juice
- 3 garlic cloves, minced
- 1¼ tsp za'atar
- ½ tsp agave nectar
- ½ tsp ground cumin
- ½ tsp kosher salt
- ¼ tsp black pepper

FOR THE SALAD

- 2 medium heads of romaine lettuce, about 14oz (400g), chopped
- ¾ cup sliced mini cucumber
- ½ cup pomegranate arils
- 3 mandarin oranges, supremed (see note)
- ¼ cup pickled red onion (see page 251)
- ⅓ cup roasted salted pistachios, chopped
- 2 tbsp thinly sliced mint

1. To make the couscous, to a small pot, add ¾ cup of water and bring to a boil. Add the couscous and salt and reduce the heat to a simmer. Cover with a lid and cook for 10 to 15 minutes, until tender, then drain any remaining water. Transfer to a small bowl and set aside to cool to room temperature.
2. To make the haloumi, heat a large nonstick skillet over medium heat. Once hot, add the halloumi slices in a single layer. Cook for 2 to 3 minutes, until golden brown, then use tongs to flip and cook for another 2 to 3 minutes, until golden brown on both sides. Transfer the halloumi to a plate and set aside to cool for about 10 minutes.
3. To make the vinaigrette, in a small bowl, whisk together the olive oil, lemon juice, garlic, za'atar, agave, cumin, salt, and pepper until well combined.
4. To make the salad, in a large salad bowl or on a platter, arrange the lettuce. Top

with the couscous, halloumi, cucumbers, pomegranate arils, oranges, pickled onion, pistachios, and mint. Drizzle the dressing over top and toss lightly to coat before serving.

Make it gluten-free: Use cooked quinoa in place of the couscous.

Note: To supreme an orange (or any citrus), start by slicing off the top and bottom to expose the fruit and create two flat ends. Using a paring knife, cut off the peel and the pith (the bitter white layer under the peel), following the curve of the fruit. Lastly, carefully slice on either side of the membranes that separate the fruit into segments. Repeat this process until all the segments are removed.

Mains

STAUB
STAUB

SERVES 6 | PREP TIME: 25 MINUTES COOK TIME: 20 MINUTES

Creamy Lemon-Chicken Pasta

Lexi: I've never been a huge fan of chicken Alfredo, but I definitely understand the appeal of a good creamy pasta sauce. This version, with a lemony ricotta base, is much more my style, and it's rich and luxurious but not so heavy. Frozen peas are the easiest vegetable add-in, and I love the pop of sweet, fresh flavor they add. If you need some extra greens, broccoli is a great addition too.

- 2 tsp kosher salt, divided
- 12oz (350g) pasta of choice (casarecce, farfalle, penne, etc.)
- 2 boneless, skinless chicken breasts, 12oz (350g) total, cut into 1-inch (2.5cm) cubes
- 1 tsp lemon pepper seasoning, divided
- 2 tbsp olive oil
- 2 tbsp salted butter
- 6 garlic cloves, minced
- 2 cups whole milk
- 4oz (115g) whole-milk ricotta cheese, plus more to garnish
- ¼ cup grated Parmesan, plus more to garnish
- 1 tbsp lemon zest
- 1 cup frozen peas
- ½ cup chopped parsley, plus more to garnish
- ¼ cup freshly squeezed lemon juice

1. In a large pot, add 4 quarts of water and 1 teaspoon of the kosher salt and bring to a boil. Add the pasta and cook to al dente, uncovered, according to package instructions. Reserve ¾ cup of the pasta water, then drain the pasta and set aside.
2. Season the chicken all over with ½ teaspoon of the salt and ¼ teaspoon of the lemon pepper seasoning. To a large skillet over medium heat, add the oil. Once the oil shimmers or ripples slightly, add the chicken and cook for 5 to 7 minutes, stirring occasionally, until the chicken is lightly browned on all sides. Transfer to a plate and set aside.
3. Working with the same large skillet, reduce the heat to medium-low and add the butter. Once melted, stir in the garlic and cook for 1 minute, until fragrant.
4. Whisk in the milk, ricotta, Parmesan, lemon zest, the remaining ½ teaspoon salt, and the remaining ¾ teaspoon lemon pepper seasoning. Increase the heat to medium-high and bring the sauce to a gentle boil, then let simmer for about 1 minute.
5. Stir in the pasta, chicken, peas, parsley, lemon juice, and 2 to 3 tablespoons of the reserved pasta water. Mix well and cook for 4 to 5 minutes, stirring and tossing, until the sauce has thickened. If needed, stir in more pasta water to reach your desired consistency.
6. Serve hot with a few dollops of ricotta, a sprinkle of grated Parmesan, and a garnish of fresh parsley on top.

Make it vegetarian: Replace the chicken with an equal quantity of drained and rinsed white beans. Add them in when you stir in the pasta, peas, parsley, lemon juice, and pasta water.

SERVES 4 | PREP TIME: 15 MINUTES COOK TIME: 45 MINUTES

 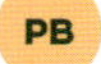

Sofritas Tofu Tacos

If you've ever had the vegetarian protein option at Chipotle (sofritas), that's essentially what this recipe is but *way* better. And if you don't love tofu, that's just because you haven't found the right recipe yet. If we had to recommend one tofu recipe for the tofu skeptics, it would be this one. The secret is that we start by baking the tofu in small pieces until it's super crispy, then we chop it up and cook it again in a flavorful spicy adobo sauce. The end result leaves you with tofu that has a very meaty texture, lots of crispy edges, and so much flavor in every single bite. It makes for an excellent vegetarian taco, but you can also use it in burritos, burrito bowls, quesadillas, and more.

FOR THE TOFU

14oz (400g) extra-firm tofu, drained, sliced in half widthwise, and pressed (see note), then diced into ½-inch (1cm) cubes
1 tbsp avocado or vegetable oil
1 tbsp cornstarch
½ tsp kosher salt

FOR THE SAUCE

1 chipotle pepper in adobo sauce, plus 1–2 tbsp adobo sauce, to taste
2 tbsp tomato paste
1½ tbsp freshly squeezed lime juice
1 tsp sugar or agave nectar
1 tsp kosher salt
¾ tsp dried oregano
½ tsp ground cumin
½ tsp ground coriander
2 tbsp avocado or vegetable oil
1 cup diced yellow onion
1 tbsp minced garlic

FOR SERVING

8 small corn tortillas, warmed
1 avocado, thinly sliced or diced
Pickled red onions (see page 251)
Crumbled queso fresco (optional)
Chopped cilantro

1. Preheat the oven to 375°F (190°C). Line a sheet pan with parchment paper.
2. To make the tofu, in a plastic ziplock or reusable bag, place the tofu cubes and oil and shake to coat. Add the cornstarch and salt, then shake again until evenly coated.
3. On the prepared sheet pan, spread the tofu out evenly and bake for 25 to 30 minutes, stirring halfway through, until golden brown and crispy. Remove from the oven, let cool slightly, then roughly chop into smaller pieces. Set aside.
4. To make the sauce, in a blender, combine the chipotle pepper and adobo sauce, tomato paste, lime juice, sugar, salt, oregano, cumin, coriander, and ½ cup of water and blend until smooth.
5. To a large skillet over medium heat, add the oil. Once hot, add the onion and cook for 5 minutes, stirring occasionally, until softened and translucent. Stir in the garlic and cook for 1 minute, continuing to stir, until fragrant. Add the chopped tofu and the blended sauce and mix well. Let cook for 10 to 15 minutes, stirring occasionally, until the sauce has mostly reduced and the tofu is crispy.
6. To serve, spoon the tofu into warmed or charred tortillas with the avocado, pickled onion, queso fresco (if using), and chopped cilantro, or any other toppings of choice.

Note: Pressing tofu helps with extracting as much liquid as possible. Wrap the tofu block with a clean tea towel or several paper towels, place on a cutting board, and set something heavy on top, like a cast-iron skillet. Let the tofu sit to drain for 30 minutes.

SERVES 4 | PREP TIME: 25 MINUTES COOK TIME: 10 MINUTES

Fish Taco Bowls
with Creamy Jalapeño-Avocado Sauce

These bowls are always a hit with the family, because they're so easy to customize with everyone's preferred toppings. We like ours with pickled cabbage for crunch and tang (see page 251), but coleslaw is another great option. We also like to add black beans for a bit more heft, extra avocado for good measure, a few jalapeño slices (fresh or quick pickled), and a sprinkle of cotija cheese. Feel free to load yours up with more fresh produce, like tomatoes, corn, or red onion. White or brown rice makes for a great base, but our Cilantro-Lime Rice (page 253) is even better. For the protein, white fish—like haddock, cod, halibut, or tilapia—is best.

FOR THE FISH

1 tsp kosher salt
1 tsp chili powder
½ tsp ground cumin
½ tsp ground coriander
½ tsp sweet paprika
½ tsp garlic powder
¼ tsp onion powder
About 4 filets of white fish, 1lb (450g) total, cut into 1-inch (2.5cm) cubes
2 tbsp avocado or vegetable oil, plus more as needed

FOR THE CREAMY JALAPEÑO-AVOCADO SAUCE

1 medium avocado
3 tbsp freshly squeezed lime juice
2 tbsp sour cream
2 tbsp minced jalapeño, seeds removed
1 tbsp chopped cilantro
1 tsp honey
1 garlic clove, minced
½ tsp kosher salt

FOR SERVING

Cooked white rice or Cilantro-Lime Rice (page 253)
Pickled cabbage (see page 251)
Black beans, drained and rinsed
Sliced avocado
Sliced jalapeño, fresh or pickled (optional; see page 251)
Crumbled cotija cheese (optional)

1. To make the fish, in a small bowl, stir together the salt, chili powder, cumin, coriander, paprika, garlic powder, and onion powder. To a large bowl, add the fish and generously season, gently stirring with a spatula, until well coated.
2. Heat a large nonstick pan over medium-high heat and add the oil. Once the oil shimmers or ripples slightly, add half of the fish. Sear on one side for 2 to 3 minutes, until browned and crispy, then flip and sear for another 2 to 3 minutes, until crispy and cooked to an internal temperature of 145°F (63°C). Using tongs or a slotted spoon, carefully remove the fish from the pan and transfer to a plate. Add more oil to the pan if needed and repeat with the second batch of fish. Set the fish aside.
3. To make the jalapeño-avocado sauce, to a blender, add the avocado, lime juice, sour cream, jalapeño, cilantro, honey, garlic, salt, and 3 tablespoons of water and blend until completely

smooth. If needed, add an additional 1 to 2 tablespoons of water for a pourable consistency.

4. To serve, assemble the bowls with rice, fish, pickled cabbage, black beans, avocado, jalapeño (if using), and cotija cheese (if using). Drizzle with the jalapeño-avocado sauce before serving.

Make it dairy-free: Swap the sour cream with your favorite plant-based alternative and leave out the cotija cheese.

SERVES 6 | **PREP TIME:** 15 MINUTES, PLUS MARINATING TIME **COOK TIME:** 25 MINUTES

Citrus-Herb Chicken Kebabs

DF

Lexi: I could happily eat this chicken, and only this chicken, for the rest of my life. The marinade is absolutely packed with flavor, thanks to three types of citrus juice and zest, Dijon mustard, honey, and all sorts of spices. Citrus helps to tenderize the chicken, so it stays moist and tender even after getting a good char on the exterior. Make sure to let the chicken marinate for at least 2 hours, but ideally 6 hours or overnight for maximum flavor. You can also grill the chicken breasts whole, but cubing the chicken allows for more surface area to soak up the sweet-and-sour citrus flavor.

½ cup freshly squeezed orange juice
⅓ cup olive oil
¼ cup freshly squeezed lemon juice
2 tbsp freshly squeezed lime juice
2 tbsp finely chopped parsley
1 tbsp soy sauce
1 tbsp Dijon mustard
1 tbsp honey
2 tsp kosher salt
2 tsp dried oregano
1 tbsp orange zest
1½ tsp lemon zest
1 tsp onion powder
¾ tsp garlic powder
¾ tsp smoked paprika
½ tsp ground cumin
¼ tsp ground black pepper
6 boneless, skinless chicken breasts, about 6oz (175g) each, diced into 1½-inch (3.8cm) cubes
8–10 wooden or metal skewers

1. In a medium bowl, whisk together the orange juice, olive oil, lemon juice, lime juice, parsley, soy sauce, Dijon mustard, honey, salt, oregano, orange zest, lemon zest, onion powder, garlic powder, paprika, cumin, and black pepper.
2. In a gallon-size ziplock bag, add the chicken and pour in the marinade. Seal the bag, removing as much air as possible, and gently massage the chicken to evenly coat it with the marinade. Refrigerate and let marinate for at least 2 hours or overnight.
3. If using wooden skewers, soak in water for 20 minutes before skewering to prevent burning.
4. Preheat the grill to medium-high heat. Thread the skewers with the marinated chicken pieces so they are touching, about 6 to 8 pieces per skewer. Reserve the leftover marinade for basting during cooking.
5. Grill the skewers for about 20 minutes, turning several times to ensure the chicken cooks evenly on all sides. Halfway through cooking, baste the chicken with the reserved marinade, then discard the remaining marinade.
6. Remove the skewers from the grill and let rest for 5 to 10 minutes, then serve and enjoy.

SERVES 6 | **PREP TIME: 30 MINUTES** **COOK TIME: 30 MINUTES**

GF DF

Peach-Barbecue Grilled Chicken

As soon as peach season comes around, you can bet we're going to stock up on as many as we possibly can find. Inevitably, there are always a few that end up a little too bruised for snacking, but they're perfect for our smoky, sweet, tangy peach-barbecue sauce. It's honestly good enough that you'll want to lick the spoon. You can use the sauce for ribs, pulled pork, or baked beans, but our go-to application is grilled chicken. It's delicious paired with other summertime favorites, like our Zucchini Corn Fritters (page 164) or Cucumber, Basil, and Avocado Gazpacho (page 78).

FOR THE PEACH-BARBECUE SAUCE

2 tsp olive oil
3 tbsp minced shallot
2 garlic cloves, minced
1 cup peeled and diced peaches (see notes)
2 tbsp light brown sugar, packed
3 tbsp ketchup
1 tbsp apple cider vinegar
½ tbsp gluten-free Worcestershire sauce
½ tbsp Dijon mustard
½ tsp smoked paprika
¼ tsp ground black pepper
¼ tsp kosher salt
⅛ tsp ground cumin
⅛ tsp ground ginger
Pinch of cayenne pepper (optional)

FOR THE CHICKEN

High-heat oil (like avocado or sunflower oil), for greasing the grill
2 tsp light brown sugar, packed
1½ tsp kosher salt
1½ tsp smoked paprika
¾ tsp garlic powder
¾ tsp onion powder
½ tsp ground black pepper
⅛ tsp ground ginger
⅛ tsp ground cumin
6 boneless, skinless chicken breasts, about 6oz (175g) each

1. Preheat the grill to medium-high heat and lightly oil the grates by pouring high-heat oil on a paper towel and using tongs to rub the paper towel directly on the grill grates.
2. To make the peach-barbecue sauce, to a small skillet over medium heat, add the olive oil. When the oil is hot and shimmers or slightly ripples, add the shallot and cook for 3 minutes, stirring occasionally, until softened. Add the garlic and cook for an additional 2 minutes, until fragrant. Stir in the peaches and brown sugar and cook for 5 minutes, stirring often, until the peaches have softened.
3. To a blender, add the ketchup, apple cider vinegar, Worcestershire sauce, Dijon mustard, paprika, black pepper, salt, cumin, ginger, cayenne pepper (if using), and the cooked peach mixture. To ensure safe blending, use a heat-safe blender or slightly crack the lid away from you to allow steam to release. Blend until smooth, scraping down the sides as needed to fully incorporate the ingredients. Transfer half of the barbecue sauce to a separate bowl. Set both aside.

4. To make the chicken, in a small bowl, mix together the brown sugar, salt, paprika, garlic powder, onion powder, black pepper, ginger, and cumin. With this spice mixture, season both sides of each chicken breast, rubbing it in so it sticks.
5. Grill the chicken for about 6 minutes, until it begins to develop well-defined grill marks. Flip and generously baste the cooked side with the peach-barbecue sauce from the blender. Grill for another 6 minutes, until grill marks develop. Flip again and baste the top of the chicken with the barbecue sauce. Grill for 3 to 4 minutes more on each side, basting the top of the chicken each time, until the chicken reaches an internal temperature of 165°F (75°C).
6. Let the chicken rest for 5 to 10 minutes. Serve warm with the reserved peach-barbecue sauce.

Notes: If you have extra time, cover and refrigerate the dry-rubbed chicken for 2 hours. Let it come to room temperature before grilling.

To peel the skin off the peaches, use a vegetable peeler.

SERVES 6 | PREP TIME: 30 MINUTES COOK TIME: 40 MINUTES

GF

Sheet-Pan Clam Bake

A clam bake is one of our family's annual late-summer traditions, and it's an all-hands-on-deck affair. Grandpa performs quality assurance on the clams and oversees the whole production, cousins husk the corn, Dad peels the potatoes, and the ladies sit back and enjoy a cocktail. This recipe is a way, way simpler version of our much more complicated clam bake, during which we cook everything in a large metal trash can over the fire pit. This utilizes a sheet pan and an oven instead, and the clams are all doused in a garlicky Old Bay butter sauce. Serve it up family-style right on the sheet pans with a cold beer (or rosé, if you want to get fancy).

FOR THE CLAM BAKE

1 tbsp kosher salt
1½lb (675g) baby red potatoes
4 ears of corn, cut into 3-inch (7.5cm) pieces
24 littleneck clams
16–20 raw shell-on shrimp, about 1½lb (675g) total
12oz (350g) andouille chicken sausage, sliced ½ inch (1cm) thick
Finely chopped parsley, to garnish
1 large lemon, cut into 8 wedges, to garnish

FOR THE GARLICKY OLD BAY BUTTER SAUCE

¾ cup salted butter
½ cup dry white wine
½ cup minced shallots
½ cup finely chopped parsley
1½ tbsp Old Bay seasoning
1 tbsp freshly squeezed lemon juice
3 garlic cloves, minced

1. Position one rack in the middle of the oven and another in the lower third, and preheat to 425°F (220°C).
2. To a large pot over high heat, add 3 quarts of water and the salt and bring to a boil. Then reduce the heat slightly and add the potatoes. Cook for 15 minutes, until the potatoes are fork tender, then drain and set aside.
3. To make the butter sauce, in a small pot over medium heat, melt the butter, then whisk in the wine, shallots, parsley, Old Bay seasoning, lemon juice, and garlic. Cook for 1 to 2 minutes, whisking continuously, until the alcohol has cooked off and the sauce is smooth. Remove from the heat.
4. To make the clam bake, to a large bowl, add the cooked potatoes, corn, clams, shrimp, and sausage. Pour the butter sauce over top and toss until all ingredients are well coated.
5. Divide the mixture evenly over two large sheet pans. Place both sheet pans on the middle rack of the oven if they fit or one on the middle and one on the lower rack. Bake for about 20 minutes, until the shrimp are opaque and the clams have opened. If your sheet pans are on separate racks, rotate them halfway through cooking, and note that the clams and shrimp may need an extra 5 to 10 minutes of cooking time. (After the maximum cooking time, discard any clams that haven't opened.)
6. Serve family style, garnished with the parsley and lemon wedges.

SERVES 4 | PREP TIME: 10 MINUTES COOK TIME: 20 MINUTES

Pan-Seared Scallops
with Burst Cherry Tomatoes and Basil

Beth: I'm not usually huge on seafood, but I'll never pass up a perfectly seared, buttery, tender scallop. One of the best parts about making scallops at home is that they only take a few minutes to cook, and as long as your pan is nice and hot and your scallops are patted dry, you'll be able to sear them just as beautifully as your local seafood restaurant. Paired with blistered, jammy cherry tomatoes, briny capers, garlic, and white wine, this recipe is ideal for a late summer evening, when tomatoes are at their peak. Enjoy with crusty bread, pasta, or cooked polenta as a side, and a crisp glass of sauvignon blanc.

1½lb (675g) large scallops, side muscles removed, patted dry
1 tsp kosher salt, plus more to taste
¼ tsp ground black pepper, plus more to taste
3 tbsp olive or avocado oil
3 tbsp salted butter
¼ cup finely diced shallots
3 garlic cloves, minced
1½ tsp lemon zest
1lb (450g) cherry tomatoes
½ cup dry white wine
1½ tbsp freshly squeezed lemon juice
¼ cup finely chopped basil
1 tbsp capers, drained
¼ tsp red pepper flakes
Grated Parmesan, to serve (optional)

1. Season the scallops with the salt and pepper on both sides. Heat a large stainless-steel skillet over medium-high heat and add the oil. Once the oil shimmers or ripples slightly, add the scallops, making sure not to overcrowd the pan. If needed, cook in two batches. Sear the scallops for 2 to 3 minutes, undisturbed, until they form a golden-brown crust and release from the pan easily. Flip and sear for another 2 to 3 minutes, until the other side is golden brown and the internal temperature reaches 115°F (46°C). Transfer to a plate and set aside.
2. Reduce the heat to medium-low and add the butter. Once melted, add the shallots and cook for 2 to 3 minutes, stirring often, until softened and fragrant. Add the garlic and lemon zest and cook for 30 seconds, until fragrant.
3. Stir in the cherry tomatoes and season with additional salt and pepper to taste. Increase the heat to medium and cook for about 5 minutes, stirring occasionally, until the tomatoes start to burst and become jammy.
4. Stir in the white wine and lemon juice and cook for 1 to 2 minutes, until simmering. Add the basil, capers, and red pepper flakes. Cook for 2 to 3 more minutes, stirring occasionally, until the basil is wilted, then return the scallops to the skillet, spooning some of the sauce over them. Remove from the heat and serve hot with a sprinkle of Parmesan (if using).

MAKES 6 | **PREP TIME:** 20 MINUTES **COOK TIME:** 35 MINUTES

Turkey Burgers
with Blueberry Compote and Jalapeño-Basil Aioli

Don't be scared off by the fact that these are made with turkey, because we promise, these are far from the dry, bland turkey burger you're imagining. The burger patty itself is surprisingly juicy, moist, and flavorful, thanks to a few secret ingredients: grated onion, Dijon mustard, and Worcestershire sauce. We like to make an extra batch and chop them up for an easy protein source to add to other meals. Blueberry compote might sound like an unusual burger topping, but paired with a spicy, herby aioli, peppery arugula, and creamy Havarti cheese, it makes for a truly delicious, unique burger.

FOR THE BLUEBERRY COMPOTE

2 cups fresh or frozen blueberries
1 tbsp freshly squeezed lime juice
1 tbsp light brown sugar
2 tsp cornstarch
¼ tsp kosher salt
Ground black pepper, to taste

FOR THE JALAPEÑO-BASIL AIOLI

½ cup mayonnaise
3 tbsp finely chopped basil
2 tbsp minced jalapeño, seeds removed
1 tsp garlic powder
1 tsp freshly squeezed lime juice
Kosher salt, to taste

FOR THE BURGERS

2lb (900g) ground turkey
½ cup grated yellow onion
2 tbsp mayonnaise
2 tsp Worcestershire sauce
2 tsp Dijon mustard
2 tsp kosher salt
½ tsp ground black pepper
½ tsp garlic powder
Olive or avocado oil
6 slices of Havarti cheese

FOR SERVING

6 buns of choice, toasted
Arugula

1. To make the blueberry compote, in a small saucepan over medium heat, combine the blueberries, lime juice, brown sugar, cornstarch, salt, and pepper to taste. Stir well and bring to a simmer, then reduce the heat to medium-low and simmer for 4 to 5 minutes, gently mashing the blueberries with a wooden spoon, until the mixture starts to thicken slightly. Transfer to a bowl and let cool to room temperature.
2. To make the aioli, in a small bowl, stir together the mayonnaise, basil, jalapeño, garlic powder, lime juice, and salt until combined. Set aside in the refrigerator until ready to use.
3. To make the burgers, in a large bowl, combine the ground turkey, onion, mayonnaise, Worcestershire sauce, Dijon mustard, salt, pepper, and garlic powder. Using your hands or a spatula, mix until all ingredients are evenly incorporated. Form into six 6-ounce (175g) patties that are about the same diameter as the buns.
4. Heat a large skillet over medium-high heat and add just enough oil to lightly coat the bottom of the pan. Once the oil is hot and

shimmers or ripples slightly, place two patties in the pan. Cook for 4 to 6 minutes, until browned, then flip the patties. Top each with a slice of Havarti cheese, then cover with a lid and cook for another 4 to 6 minutes, until the internal temperature of the patty reaches 160°F (70°C) and the cheese is melted. Transfer to a plate and repeat with the remaining patties. (If you prefer to grill the burgers instead, see note.)

5. To assemble the burgers, on each bottom bun, spread about 1 tablespoon of the aioli. Top with a patty, then about 1 tablespoon of the blueberry compote and a small handful of arugula. Finish with the top bun and enjoy warm.

Note: To grill the burgers, preheat the grill to 400°F (200°C). Once hot, cook the burgers for about 6 minutes on one side, until grill marks form. Flip the burgers and cook for another 4 minutes. Then top with the cheese slices and cook for a final 2 minutes, until the patty reaches an internal temperature of 160°F (70°C). Remove from the grill and let rest for 5 minutes before assembling and serving.

SERVES 4 | PREP TIME: 10 MINUTES, PLUS MARINATING TIME COOK TIME: 13 MINUTES

Sweet and Smoky Glazed Salmon with Mango-Grapefruit Salsa

A simple but flavorful pantry glaze makes for a beautifully caramelized filet of salmon that comes together quickly and easily in the oven. This is one of those recipes that's simple enough for a busy Tuesday but also makes for a great dinner party main. It's topped with a fruit-based salsa that brings a whole lot of freshness to the party. If you're not a fan of grapefruit, try oranges instead. Pineapple is another great addition, or works as a replacement for mango. We prefer to use wild sockeye salmon, but any kind will do.

FOR THE SALMON

1 salmon filet, about 2lb (900g), skin on, patted dry
1 tbsp olive oil
3 tbsp light brown sugar
1 ½ tsp smoked paprika
¾ tsp onion powder
¾ tsp kosher salt
¼ tsp ground black pepper

FOR THE MANGO-GRAPEFRUIT SALSA

2 grapefruits, peeled, supremed (see note on page 121), and diced
1 ripe mango, peeled and finely diced
1 large avocado, finely diced
1 large jalapeño, seeds removed and finely diced
¼ cup diced red onion
2 tbsp chopped cilantro
2 tbsp freshly squeezed lime juice
½ tsp kosher salt
¼ tsp chili powder
¼ tsp ground black pepper

1. Preheat the oven to 400°F (200°C). Line a sheet pan with parchment paper.
2. To prepare the salmon, place the salmon filet on the prepared sheet pan. Brush the top of the salmon with the olive oil in an even layer.
3. In a small bowl, combine the brown sugar, paprika, onion powder, salt, and pepper. Stir to combine, then sprinkle evenly on top of the salmon. Cover and refrigerate for 30 minutes to marinate. (This step can be skipped if short on time.)
4. To make the salsa, in a medium bowl, combine the grapefruit, mango, avocado, jalapeño, onion, cilantro, lime juice, salt, chili powder, and pepper and stir.
5. Bake the salmon for 5 minutes, then set the oven to broil and broil for 5 to 8 minutes, keeping a close eye on your oven to prevent burning, until the fish is golden brown on top and cooked to 140°F (60°C) in the center.
6. Serve warm with the mango-grapefruit salsa spooned over top.

SERVES 4 | PREP TIME: 15 MINUTES COOK TIME: 35 MINUTES

Garlicky Shrimp and Chorizo

over Cheesy Manchego Polenta

This is the type of recipe that's big on flavor but low on effort. Polenta is one of our favorite easy grains—it takes about 20 minutes to make, and it's pretty hard to mess up. The shrimp sears in just a few minutes, and the chorizo adds plenty of flavor and spice. Manchego is a Spanish sheep-milk cheese that's mildly sweet, nutty, and salty. It adds so much flavor to the polenta with minimal work. If you can't find any, try a mixture of Parmesan and mild white cheddar instead.

FOR THE POLENTA

1½ tsp kosher salt, plus more to taste
1½ cups polenta
3 tbsp salted butter
1 cup finely shredded Manchego cheese

FOR THE SHRIMP AND CHORIZO

8oz (225g) raw chorizo
3 tbsp olive oil, divided
31–35 raw large shrimp, about 1lb (450g) total, peeled and deveined
1 tsp dried oregano
¾ tsp sweet paprika
¼ tsp kosher salt, plus more to taste
¼ tsp red pepper flakes, plus more to taste
½ cup minced shallots
¼ cup oil-packed sun-dried tomatoes, drained and chopped
5 garlic cloves, minced
⅓ cup dry sherry
½ cup chicken or vegetable broth
2oz (60g) halved green olives
2 tbsp chopped parsley, plus more to garnish
Juice of ½ a lemon
Shaved Manchego cheese, to garnish (optional)

1. To make the polenta, in a medium pot, combine 5 cups of water and the salt and bring to a boil. While whisking constantly, pour the polenta into the boiling water. Reduce the heat to low and let simmer, whisking occasionally, for 5 minutes, until the polenta has started to absorb some of the water.
2. Stir in the butter, cover with a lid, and cook for 15 minutes, whisking occasionally, until the polenta is tender. Stir in the cheese until melted, then remove from the heat when the polenta is soft and creamy, with a texture similar to porridge. Taste and season with more salt as needed.
3. To make the shrimp and chorizo, to a large skillet over medium heat, add the raw chorizo and cook for 5 to 6 minutes, breaking it apart with a wooden spoon, until browned and crispy. With a slotted spoon, remove the cooked chorizo and set aside on a plate.
4. To the same skillet, add 1 tablespoon of the olive oil, then the shrimp, oregano, paprika, salt, and red pepper flakes. Cook for 2 to 3 minutes per side, until browned and opaque. Remove from the pan and set aside with the chorizo.
5. Reduce the heat to medium-low and add the remaining 2 tablespoons of oil. Add the shallots, sun-dried tomatoes, and garlic and cook for 2 to 3 minutes, stirring occasionally, until fragrant.
6. Pour in the sherry and let simmer for 1 minute, scraping any caramelized bits off the bottom of the pan. Stir in the chicken broth, olives, parsley, and lemon juice and bring to a simmer. Return the shrimp and chorizo to the skillet and stir to coat in the sauce. Season with more salt and red pepper flakes to taste.
7. Spoon the polenta into bowls and top with the shrimp-and-chorizo mixture. Sprinkle with the parsley and top with the shaved Manchego cheese (if using). Serve hot.

SERVES 6 | **PREP TIME:** 20 MINUTES **COOK TIME:** 30 MINUTES

Hot Honey Panko Chicken Cutlets

We like to think of this recipe as a more sophisticated version of chicken tenders. With a super crispy panko crust and just the right amount of heat, these cutlets are pan-fried to perfection and drizzled with hot honey for a sweet-and-spicy finish. The key to any good cutlet is to make sure it's thin enough, so don't be afraid to really put some muscle behind that meat mallet. These are quick and easy enough for a weeknight but special enough to serve for company. Pair them with a simple slaw or a vegetable side like our Parmesan-Crusted Brussels Sprouts (page 172). You can also chop them up for a bowl or salad topping.

3 boneless, skinless chicken breasts, about 1½lb (680g) total
½ cup all-purpose flour
1 tsp sweet paprika
½ tsp cayenne pepper
½ tsp kosher salt
¼ tsp ground black pepper
2 large eggs
2 cups panko breadcrumbs
¾ cup grated Parmesan
Vegetable or avocado oil
Homemade Hot Honey (page 255) or store bought, to serve

1. Butterfly each chicken breast by cutting it in half widthwise to make two thinner cutlets. Using a meat tenderizer, pound the chicken breasts until they're about ¼ inch (5mm) thick.
2. Gather 3 shallow bowls and a sheet pan. In one bowl, whisk together the flour, paprika, cayenne pepper, salt, and black pepper. In another bowl, whisk together the eggs and 1 tablespoon of water until smooth. In the third bowl, stir together the panko breadcrumbs and the grated Parmesan.
3. With one hand, coat a cutlet in the flour mixture and shake off any excess flour. Transfer to your other hand and coat both sides in the egg mixture, letting the excess run off, then with the same hand, transfer to the breadcrumb mixture. Using your dry hand, coat the cutlet in the breadcrumbs, pressing the crumbs into the cutlet to ensure it's completely covered. Transfer the cutlet to the sheet pan and repeat with the remaining chicken.
4. To a large, heavy-bottomed skillet over medium-low heat, add ¼ inch (5mm) of the oil and bring to about 350°F (180°C). Set a wire cooling rack on top of a clean sheet pan.
5. Once the oil is to temperature, place two cutlets into the pan. Cook for 5 to 8 minutes, until golden brown and crispy, then flip and cook for another 5 to 8 minutes, until the chicken is golden brown and crispy on both sides and the internal temperature is between 160°F and 165°F (70°C to 75°C). It's important to keep the oil around 350°F (180°C) so the chicken cooks through to the perfect golden-brown color. When they're done, transfer to the wire cooling rack. Add more oil to the skillet if needed, and repeat with the remaining cutlets.
6. Drizzle the cutlets with hot honey before serving warm.

SERVES 6 | PREP TIME: 20 MINUTES COOK TIME: 40 MINUTES

Poblano White Bean Chili

This hearty chili is always a hit in our house, even amongst family members that usually prefer their meals with meat. It's perfect for any weeknight, or a lazy Sunday when you want something nourishing and cozy but unfussy. If you want your future self to thank you, make a double batch and freeze half for up to 4 months. Let it defrost overnight in the fridge before reheating and loading up with toppings.

3 tbsp avocado or olive oil
1½ cups diced yellow onion
½ cup diced poblano pepper, seeds removed
3 garlic cloves, minced
1 large red bell pepper, diced
10oz (285g) frozen corn
One 4oz (113g) can mild green chiles
2 tbsp tomato paste
2 tsp dried oregano
1½ tsp chili powder
1 tsp ground cumin
1 tsp ground coriander
1 tsp kosher salt
½ tsp smoked paprika
6 cups vegetable broth, divided
3 tbsp all-purpose flour
Three 15½oz (439g) cans navy beans, drained and rinsed
3 tbsp chopped cilantro, plus more to garnish
1 tbsp freshly squeezed lime juice
1 cup grated white cheddar cheese, plus more to serve
Sour cream, to serve
Diced avocado, to serve
Thinly sliced radishes, to serve (optional)

1. To a large pot over medium heat, add the oil. Once the oil shimmers or ripples slightly, add the onion and poblano pepper and cook for 5 minutes, stirring occasionally, until they start to soften. Stir in the garlic and cook for another minute, until fragrant.
2. Stir in the bell pepper, corn, green chiles, tomato paste, oregano, chili powder, cumin, coriander, salt, and paprika and cook for 3 to 4 minutes, stirring occasionally, until the peppers start to soften.
3. In a medium bowl, whisk together 1 cup of the broth and the flour until smooth. Pour the flour-broth mixture into the pot along with the remaining 5 cups broth and stir. Increase the heat to high and bring the soup to a boil, then reduce the heat to medium-low and simmer uncovered for 20 minutes, stirring occasionally, until slightly thickened.
4. Add the beans, cilantro, and lime juice and cook for 10 minutes to warm through, then stir in the cheese and cook for 2 to 3 minutes more, until melted.
5. Serve hot topped with a dollop of sour cream, shredded cheese, avocado, radishes (if using), and cilantro.

Make it gluten-free: Use your favorite gluten-free 1-to-1 or measure-for-measure flour.

Make it plant-based: Leave out the cheese or use your favorite plant-based alternative.

STAUB

SERVES 6 | **PREP TIME:** 15 MINUTES **COOK TIME:** 45 MINUTES

DF

Roasted Chicken Thighs
with Pancetta and Red Grapes

Grapes may seem unusual in this, but they add just the right amount of sweetness to cut through the fat from the crispy chicken and salt from the pancetta, and they pair beautifully with a splash of sherry and balsamic vinegar. This unexpected combination is a great main dish for a fancier dinner party. You can serve it with a side of mashed potatoes, polenta, or pasta.

- 6–8 bone-in, skin-on chicken thighs, about 3lb (1.35kg) total
- 1 tbsp kosher salt, plus more to taste
- ½ tsp ground black pepper
- 4oz (115g) pancetta, diced
- 1 cup thinly sliced shallots
- 1 tbsp light brown sugar
- 1 tbsp chopped thyme
- 1½ tsp chopped rosemary
- 2 garlic cloves, minced
- ½ cup dry sherry
- 1 tbsp balsamic vinegar
- ½ cup chicken broth
- 1 tbsp all-purpose flour
- 8oz (225g) small red seedless grapes

1. Preheat the oven to 375°F (190°C).
2. Pat the chicken thighs dry with a paper towel and season both sides with the salt and pepper.
3. Heat a 12-inch (30cm) oven-safe skillet (preferably cast iron) over medium heat. Once hot, place the chicken thighs skin-side down in the skillet and cook for 5 to 6 minutes, until the skin is golden and crispy. Using tongs, flip the chicken and cook for about 3 minutes, until the bottom is lightly browned. Transfer the chicken to a plate and set aside.
4. Reduce the heat to medium-low, then add the pancetta and cook for 3 minutes, stirring occasionally, until it starts to crisp up. Stir in the shallots, brown sugar, thyme, rosemary, and a pinch of salt and cook for 3 to 4 minutes, stirring occasionally, until the shallots are softened. Add the garlic and cook for 1 minute, until fragrant.
5. Pour in the sherry and balsamic, scraping up any browned bits from the bottom of the pan. Let simmer and reduce slightly for 1 minute. Meanwhile, in a small bowl, whisk together the chicken broth and flour, then pour it into the pan, stir well, and cook for 1 to 2 minutes to thicken slightly.
6. Nestle the chicken thighs back into the skillet, skin-side up, and scatter the grapes around them. Transfer the skillet to the oven and roast for 25 to 30 minutes, until the internal temperature of the chicken reaches 165°F (75°C) in the thickest part.
7. Let the chicken rest for 5 minutes before serving.

Make it gluten-free: Use your favorite gluten-free 1-to-1 or measure-for-measure flour.

Note: If time allows, season the chicken with salt and pepper and let it marinate in the refrigerator for 6 to 8 hours (or overnight) before cooking. About 30 minutes before cooking, remove the chicken from the refrigerator.

MAKES 6 | **PREP TIME: 20 MINUTES, PLUS CHILLING TIME** **COOK TIME: 1 HOUR 10 MINUTES**

Lentil Meatball Subs

We made a sandwich to get the same saucy, cheesy satisfaction you'd expect from a classic meatball sub, minus the meat. We've been making these lentil meatballs for years. We usually keep it simple and serve them up spaghetti-and-meatball style, but we knew they were meant for something more. Moist and tender on the inside and crisp on the outside, they hold up well to as much marinara as your heart desires. Mozzarella will work just as well as provolone, and you can use shredded or sliced.

FOR THE LENTIL MEATBALLS

1 cup brown or green lentils, rinsed in cold water
3 tbsp olive oil, divided
½ cup chopped shallots
2 garlic cloves, minced
¾ cup panko breadcrumbs
⅓ cup grated Parmesan
2 tbsp finely chopped parsley
½ tbsp dried oregano
½ tbsp dried basil
1½ tsp kosher salt
¼ tsp ground black pepper
1 large egg plus 1 large egg white, lightly beaten
1½ tbsp tomato paste

FOR ASSEMBLY

1½–2 cups marinara sauce
6 hoagie rolls, sliced in half lengthwise
3 tbsp olive oil
12 slices of provolone cheese
⅓ cup grated Parmesan, to garnish
Chopped parsley, to garnish

1. Preheat the oven to 375°F (190°C). Line a sheet pan with parchment paper.
2. To make the lentil meatballs, to a medium saucepan over medium-high heat, add the rinsed lentils and 3 cups of water. Bring to a boil, then reduce the heat to low and simmer uncovered for 25 to 30 minutes, until the lentils are tender. Remove from the heat and drain any excess water. Set aside.
3. In a small skillet over medium heat, add 1 tablespoon of the olive oil. Once the oil is shimmering, add the shallots and cook, stirring often, for 3 to 4 minutes, until softened. Add the garlic and cook for 1 minute, until fragrant.
4. In a medium bowl, stir together the breadcrumbs, Parmesan, parsley, oregano, basil, salt, and pepper. To the bowl of a food processor, add the cooked lentils, cooked shallot mixture, 1½ tablespoons olive oil, breadcrumb mixture, egg and egg white, and tomato paste. Pulse several times until the mixture is well combined but still has some texture.
5. Refrigerate the lentil mixture for 20 minutes, then use a 2-tablespoon scoop to portion the meatballs. With your hands, roll each portion into a ball. Transfer to the prepared sheet pan and brush with ½ tablespoon olive oil.
6. Bake for 12 minutes, then using tongs, carefully flip the meatballs over, brush with more olive oil, and bake for about 12 minutes, until lightly browned. Remove from the oven and leave the oven on.
7. To make the sandwiches, in a large skillet over medium-low heat, combine the cooked meatballs and marinara sauce, stirring gently to coat the meatballs, and cook for about 5 minutes, until warmed.
8. Brush the interior of each hoagie roll with the olive oil and place on a sheet pan, cut-side up. Toast in the oven for 5 to 8 minutes, until golden brown. Remove from the oven and leave the oven on.
9. On each roll, place 3 or 4 meatballs with the sauce, then top with 2 slices of the provolone. Return the sandwiches to the oven for 5 minutes or until the cheese is melted. Sprinkle with the grated Parmesan and parsley and serve right away.

STAUB

SERVES 4–6 | **PREP TIME:** 30 MINUTES **COOK TIME:** 35 MINUTES

Creamy Tahini Pasta
with Feta Chicken Meatballs

One of the things we love most about this pasta is that it's simultaneously rich, creamy, and luxurious and also bright, fresh, and tangy. Plenty of feta and lemon juice cut through the nutty tahini for just the right amount of zing. The star of the show, however, is the mini chicken meatballs. Flavorful, savory, and lemony, thanks to the za'atar, they're good enough that you might want to make a double batch and save the leftovers to add to lunch or dinner the next day. Don't forget to reserve the pasta water—it's an essential component of this recipe!

FOR THE MEATBALLS

1lb (450g) ground chicken
½ cup crumbled feta cheese
⅓ cup panko breadcrumbs
¼ cup minced shallots
3 tbsp chopped parsley
2 tbsp olive oil
4 tsp za'atar
2 tsp tomato paste
1 tsp dried oregano
¾ tsp kosher salt
½ tsp garlic powder
¼ tsp ground black pepper

FOR THE PASTA

Salt, to taste
1lb (450g) orecchiette
3 tbsp olive oil, divided
⅓ cup tahini
⅓ cup crumbled feta cheese, plus more to garnish
¼ cup freshly squeezed lemon juice
1 tsp kosher salt
Ground black pepper, to taste
3 garlic cloves, minced
1½ cups baby spinach, packed and roughly chopped
¼ cup chopped parsley, plus more to garnish
Red pepper flakes (optional)

1. Preheat the oven to 350°F (180°C). Line a sheet pan with parchment paper.
2. To make the meatballs, in a medium bowl, combine the ground chicken, feta, panko breadcrumbs, shallots, parsley, olive oil, za'atar, tomato paste, oregano, salt, garlic powder, and pepper. Stir, or use your hands to mix, until well incorporated.
3. Using a tablespoon to portion the meatballs, roll each one into a ball and place on the prepared sheet pan. Bake for 20 to 22 minutes, flipping halfway through, until browned and cooked through. Set aside.
4. To make the pasta, bring a large pot of salted water to a boil. Cook the pasta according to package instructions. Before draining, reserve 2 cups of the hot pasta water.
5. In a large bowl, whisk together 2 tablespoons of the olive oil with the tahini, feta, lemon juice, salt, pepper, and 1¾ cups of the reserved pasta water until smooth.
6. In a large skillet over medium heat, add the remaining tablespoon olive oil. Once shimmering, add the garlic and cook for 1 to 2 minutes, stirring often, until fragrant. Stir in the spinach and parsley and cook for 1 minute, stirring occasionally, then add in the cooked pasta, meatballs, and tahini sauce, stirring until everything is well coated. Cook for 2 to 3 minutes, stirring occasionally, until the sauce thickens slightly. If needed, add the additional ¼ cup of water to reach your desired consistency.
7. Serve hot topped with more feta, parsley, and red pepper flakes (if using).

Make it gluten-free: Use your favorite gluten-free pasta in any shape, and gluten-free breadcrumbs for the meatballs.

SERVES 8 | **PREP TIME:** 20 MINUTES **COOK TIME:** 1 HOUR

Leek, Mushroom, and White Bean Biscuit Pot Pie

Beth: When it comes to comfort food, at the top of my list are mac and cheese, lasagna, and pot pie. This pot pie is fully vegetarian but doesn't skimp on flavor or richness. All the usual filling suspects are here—carrots, celery, and peas—with the addition of leeks, kale, mushrooms for meatiness, and navy beans in place of chicken. The homemade biscuits are flaky, buttery, and surprisingly easy to make, but we absolutely won't judge if you use store-bought instead to cut back on prep time.

FOR THE BISCUITS

3½ cups all-purpose flour, plus more for dusting
1 tbsp baking powder
1 tbsp granulated sugar
1½ tsp kosher salt
¼ tsp baking soda
1 cup unsalted butter, cold and cut into cubes
1 cup chilled buttermilk, plus more if needed and to glaze

FOR THE FILLING

⅓ cup salted butter
1 large leek, halved and thinly sliced, white and light-green parts only
3 garlic cloves, minced
1lb (450g) cremini mushrooms, sliced
1 cup sliced celery
¾ cup sliced carrots
1½ tbsp chopped thyme
1¼ tsp kosher salt
½ tsp ground black pepper
¼ cup dry white wine
Two 15½oz (439g) cans navy beans, drained and rinsed
1½ cups Tuscan kale, chopped
¾ cup frozen peas
½ cup whole milk
¼ cup all-purpose flour
2 tbsp Dijon mustard
2 cups vegetable broth

1. Preheat the oven to 400°F (200°C).
2. To make the biscuits, in a large bowl, whisk together the flour, baking powder, sugar, salt, and baking soda. Using a pastry cutter or your hands, incorporate the butter until the pieces are about the size of peas.
3. Stirring with a fork or spatula, slowly add in the buttermilk until a shaggy dough forms. If too dry, add another 1 to 2 tablespoons of buttermilk. With your hands, lightly knead the dough until it mostly comes together.
4. On a lightly floured surface, pat the dough into a 1-inch-thick (2.5cm) rectangle, then fold the dough in half lengthwise, then again into quarters. Flatten it back into a 1-inch-thick (2.5cm) rectangle, then repeat this process one more time, finishing with a 1-inch-thick (2.5cm) rectangle. Using a round 2-inch (5cm) cutter, cut the biscuits to make 8 total. Transfer to a plate and refrigerate while making the pot pie filling.

5. To make the filling, in a 12-inch (30cm) oven-safe skillet over medium heat, melt the butter. Add the leek and cook for 3 minutes, stirring occasionally, until softened. Stir in the garlic and cook for 1 minute, until fragrant.
6. Add the mushrooms and cook for 4 to 5 minutes, stirring occasionally, until they start to release moisture. Stir in the celery, carrots, thyme, salt, and pepper and cook for 5 minutes, stirring occasionally, until the vegetables are softened.
7. Pour in the wine and let simmer for 1 minute before stirring in the navy beans, kale, and peas. Cook for about 2 minutes, stirring occasionally, until the kale is wilted.
8. In a small bowl, whisk together the milk, flour, and Dijon mustard until no lumps remain. Add the milk mixture and the broth to the pan, stir to combine, and bring to a simmer for 3 to 4 minutes, until the mixture starts to thicken. Remove from the heat.
9. Top the pot pie with the chilled biscuits, spacing them evenly apart. Brush the tops of the biscuits with the buttermilk, then bake for 26 to 30 minutes, until golden brown on top. Let cool in the pan for 10 minutes before serving.

SERVES 8 | **PREP TIME:** 45 MINUTES, PLUS COOLING TIME **COOK TIME:** 1 HOUR 10 MINUTES

White Spinach and Mushroom Lasagna

Lexi: Growing up, lasagna was always the meal I was most excited for Mom to make. And honestly, I feel like that's not a particularly hot take—what's not to love about cheese, pasta, and meat sauce? It's still one of my favorites, but instead of always opting for the classic version, I like to switch things up sometimes with this White Spinach and Mushroom Lasagna. It's equally comforting and cheesy, but with a white sauce instead of red, a flavorful spinach-mushroom filling, and layers of creamy ricotta.

FOR THE WHITE SAUCE

3 tbsp unsalted butter
¼ cup all-purpose flour
3 cups whole milk
1 cup shredded mozzarella cheese
¼ cup grated Parmesan
¼ tsp ground nutmeg
¼ tsp kosher salt
Pinch of ground black pepper

FOR THE SPINACH-MUSHROOM FILLING

1 tbsp olive oil
1 cup diced yellow onion
3 garlic cloves, minced
1lb (450g) sliced white button mushrooms
2 tsp white wine vinegar
1½ tsp Italian seasoning blend
½ tsp kosher salt
¼ tsp ground black pepper
10oz (285g) baby spinach
¼ cup finely chopped parsley

FOR THE RICOTTA FILLING

1lb (450g) whole-milk ricotta cheese
¼ cup grated Parmesan
2 large eggs, lightly beaten
½ tsp Italian seasoning blend
½ tsp kosher salt
¼ tsp ground black pepper

FOR ASSEMBLY

12 sheets of no-boil lasagna noodles
2 cups shredded mozzarella cheese
¼ cup grated Parmesan

1. Preheat the oven to 350°F (180°C).
2. To make the white sauce, in a medium saucepan over medium heat, melt the butter. Whisk in the flour and cook, whisking constantly, for 1 to 2 minutes, until the butter begins to smell nutty. Gradually pour in the milk, whisking continuously to avoid lumps. Allow the mixture to thicken between additions, cooking for 5 to 7 minutes total, until thickened and completely free of lumps.
3. Stir in the mozzarella, Parmesan, nutmeg, salt, and pepper. Cook for 2 to 3 minutes, stirring occasionally, until the cheese is melted and the sauce is smooth. Remove from the heat and set aside.
4. To make the spinach-mushroom filling, to a large skillet over medium heat, add the olive oil and onion and cook for 3 minutes, stirring occasionally, until the onion is softened and translucent. Stir in the garlic and cook for another 30 seconds, until fragrant. Then, add in the mushrooms, white wine vinegar, Italian seasoning, salt, and pepper.

Cook for 5 to 6 minutes, stirring occasionally, until the mushrooms soften and release most of their moisture.

5. Stir in the spinach and parsley, and cook for 3 to 4 minutes, stirring often, until the greens are wilted. Remove from the heat and set aside.
6. To make the ricotta filling, in a medium bowl, whisk together the ricotta, Parmesan, eggs, Italian seasoning, salt, and pepper until smooth and evenly incorporated.
7. To assemble the lasagna, on the bottom of a 9 x 13-inch (23 x 33cm) baking dish, spread a few tablespoons of the white sauce in an even layer. Top with an even layer of lasagna noodles, avoiding the noodles overlapping. Spread half of the ricotta mixture evenly over the noodles, then spread one-third of the white sauce on top. Add half of the spinach and mushroom filling on top of the white sauce in an even layer.
8. Repeat this process one more time. Top with a final layer of noodles, then spread the remaining white sauce on top. Sprinkle with the mozzarella and Parmesan.
9. Cover the baking dish loosely with aluminum foil and bake for 35 minutes. Remove the aluminum foil and bake for another 10 to 15 minutes, until the cheese is melted and golden brown on top. Let cool for at least 15 minutes, or up to 30 minutes, before slicing and serving.

SERVES 4–6 | PREP TIME: 15 MINUTES COOK TIME: 1 HOUR 20 MINUTES

PB

Mushroom Stew

This mushroom stew is fully plant-based, but it's so rich and flavorful that you won't even miss the meat. We first created this recipe after coming back from a trip to Ireland, where we fell in love with the hearty stews we enjoyed at the local pubs. At first, it was challenging to re-create that same depth of flavor without meat, but we landed on the perfect formula by combining umami-packed mushrooms with plenty of red wine, plus soy sauce and Worcestershire sauce. (If you don't eat fish, make sure the brand you buy doesn't contain anchovies.) Barley turns this stew into a full meal, but you can also leave it out and serve your stew over mashed potatoes or creamy polenta instead.

⅓ cup olive oil, divided
1 medium yellow onion, diced
1lb (450g) sliced button mushrooms
8oz (225g) sliced shiitake mushrooms
3 garlic cloves, minced
1 cup diced carrots
1 cup diced, unpeeled yellow potatoes
3 tbsp tomato paste
2 tsp dried thyme
1¼ tsp kosher salt
1 tsp dried rosemary
1 tsp sweet paprika
1 tsp packed light brown sugar
½ tsp ground black pepper
4 cups vegetable broth, divided
¼ cup all-purpose flour
¾ cup dry red wine (pinot noir, merlot, etc.)
1½ tsp plant-based Worcestershire sauce (or regular, if not making plant-based)
1 tbsp soy sauce
½ cup pearl barley
1 cup fresh or frozen green beans, cut into ½-inch (1cm) pieces
1 cup fresh or frozen peas
½ cup finely chopped parsley

1. To a large pot over medium heat, add half of the olive oil. When the oil is hot and shimmers or slightly ripples, add the onion and both mushrooms and cook for 5 to 7 minutes, stirring often, until the mushrooms soften and start to brown.
2. Add the garlic and cook for 1 to 2 minutes, stirring occasionally, until fragrant. Add the remaining olive oil and the carrots, potatoes, tomato paste, thyme, salt, rosemary, paprika, brown sugar, and pepper. Mix well to coat the vegetables, and cook for 5 minutes, stirring occasionally, until the vegetables are slightly softened.
3. Meanwhile, in a small bowl, whisk together 1 cup of the vegetable broth with the flour until no lumps remain.
4. To the pot, add the red wine and scrape up any caramelized bits that have stuck to the bottom of the pan. Add the vegetable broth mixture, the remaining 3 cups vegetable broth, the Worcestershire sauce, and soy sauce. Stir well, then increase the heat to high and bring to a boil.
5. Reduce the heat to medium-low, cover with a lid, and simmer for 45 minutes, stirring occasionally, until the vegetables are fork tender and the stew has thickened.
6. While the stew is cooking, cook the pearl barley according to package instructions. Drain any excess water.
7. After the stew has simmered for 45 minutes, stir in the green beans, peas, parsley, and cooked barley. Simmer for an additional 10 to 15 minutes, until the beans and peas are tender, then serve warm.

Sides

SERVES 6–8 | **PREP TIME: 20 MINUTES** **COOK TIME: 40 MINUTES**

Leek, Pea, and Spinach Risotto

Lexi: Apart from boxed mac and cheese, risotto is one of the first dishes my mom taught me how to make. It's her go-to carbohydrate side dish for entertaining, and she would put me in charge of monitoring and stirring in the broth while she finished prepping everything else. It looks and sounds fancy, but risotto is actually fairly easy to make. It's all about timing and patience. The key to a perfectly creamy risotto is to add the hot broth in small increments and let the rice absorb most of the liquid before adding more. This version is packed with green vegetables and finished with crème fraîche and lemon juice for a light, spring-friendly vegetarian side.

2 tbsp olive oil
1 large leek, whites and light green parts only, thinly sliced, divided
2 cups baby spinach, lightly packed, divided
4 tbsp chopped parsley, divided
4 tbsp chopped basil, divided
8oz (225g) frozen or fresh peas, divided
6 cups vegetable broth, divided
1 tbsp freshly squeezed lemon juice
2 tbsp salted butter
1½ cups arborio rice
½ tsp kosher salt
¼ tsp ground black pepper
½ cup dry white wine
½ cup finely grated Parmesan or pecorino romano
¼ cup crème fraîche (see note)

TO SERVE

Chopped parsley
Finely grated Parmesan or pecorino romano
Ground black pepper

1. To a large skillet over medium heat, add the olive oil. Once the oil shimmers or ripples slightly, add half of the leeks. Cook for 2 to 3 minutes, stirring occasionally, until the leeks start to soften.
2. Add half of the spinach, half of the parsley, half of the basil, and ½ cup of the peas. Cook for 4 to 5 minutes, stirring occasionally, until the peas are tender. Remove from the heat.
3. In a blender, combine the cooked vegetable mixture, 1 cup of the vegetable broth, and the lemon juice and blend for about 45 seconds, until smooth. Be sure to crack the lid away from you to allow the steam to escape. Set aside.
4. In a medium pot over medium heat, add the remaining 5 cups vegetable broth. It doesn't need to be boiling, just steaming hot. Keep it steaming hot over medium heat for step 6.
5. In a medium skillet over medium heat, melt the butter. Once bubbling, add the remaining leeks and cook for 2 to 3 minutes, stirring occasionally, until slightly softened. Add the arborio rice, salt, and pepper and stir to evenly coat.
6. Pour in the wine, stir well, and let cook for 1 minute, then reduce the heat to medium-low. Using a ladle, add 2 ladlefuls of the hot broth to the skillet, stirring occasionally and letting the rice absorb most of the liquid before adding another 2 ladlefuls. Repeat this process for all the broth.
7. Once all the broth has been added, stir in the blended vegetable mixture and the remaining spinach, parsley, basil, and peas. Cook for about 5 minutes, stirring occasionally, until the risotto is creamy and the rice is al dente.
8. Stir in the Parmesan and crème fraîche and serve hot, garnished with more parsley, Parmesan, and black pepper.

Note: To make a crème fraîche substitute, mix ¼ cup of softened cream cheese and 1 tablespoon of whole milk or heavy cream until smooth.

SERVES 4–6 | **PREP TIME:** 20 MINUTES, PLUS SITTING TIME **COOK TIME:** 40 MINUTES

Zucchini Corn Fritters

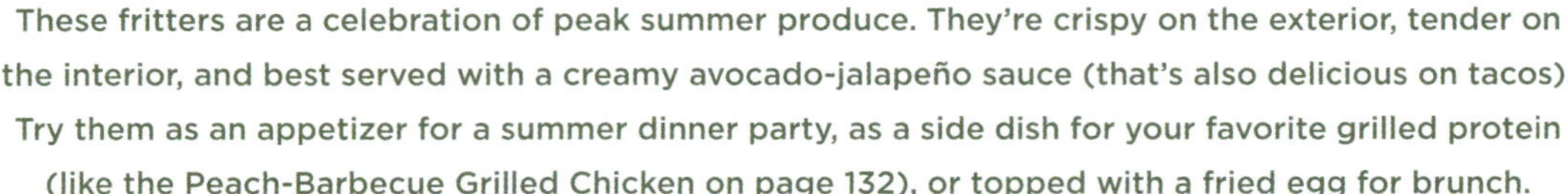
These fritters are a celebration of peak summer produce. They're crispy on the exterior, tender on the interior, and best served with a creamy avocado-jalapeño sauce (that's also delicious on tacos). Try them as an appetizer for a summer dinner party, as a side dish for your favorite grilled protein (like the Peach-Barbecue Grilled Chicken on page 132), or topped with a fried egg for brunch.

FOR THE AVOCADO-JALAPEÑO DIPPING SAUCE

½ large avocado
½ cup mayonnaise
¼ cup plain yogurt
2 tbsp freshly squeezed lime juice
2 tbsp minced jalapeño, seeds removed
2 tbsp chopped cilantro
2 tbsp chopped basil
½ tsp lime zest
½ tsp kosher salt

FOR THE FRITTERS

3 cups grated zucchini
2 tsp kosher salt, divided
2 cups fresh corn kernels
½ cup finely chopped green onion
3 tbsp finely chopped basil
2 tbsp minced jalapeño, seeds removed
2 garlic cloves, minced
1 tsp lime zest
1 cup all-purpose flour
2 tsp baking powder
⅔ cup shredded Manchego or white cheddar cheese
2 large eggs, beaten
2 tbsp neutral oil (avocado, sunflower, canola, etc.), plus more as needed

1. To make the sauce, in a small blender or food processor, combine the avocado, mayonnaise, yogurt, lime juice, jalapeño, cilantro, basil, lime zest, salt, and 3 tablespoons of water and blend until completely smooth. Transfer to the refrigerator while you make the batter.
2. To make the fritters, in a colander, toss together the zucchini and ½ teaspoon of the salt. Let sit for 30 minutes, then transfer the zucchini to a cheesecloth and squeeze out as much moisture as possible.
3. In a large bowl, combine the zucchini, corn, green onion, basil, jalapeño, garlic, and lime zest and stir to combine. In a small bowl, whisk together the flour, baking powder, and remaining 1½ teaspoons salt. Add the flour mixture to the vegetable mixture and stir to combine, then mix in the Manchego cheese and eggs until well incorporated. Let the mixture sit at room temperature for 15 minutes.
4. Line a cooling rack with a paper towel. In a large skillet over medium heat, add the oil. While the oil heats up, using a 2-tablespoon cookie dough scoop, portion out the fritter dough and shape into flat patties about ½ inch (1cm) thick.
5. When the oil is hot and shimmers or slightly ripples, working in batches of 3 or 4 fritters at a time, fry them for 3 to 4 minutes on one side, until golden brown, then carefully flip and cook for another 3 to 4 minutes, until the fritters are golden brown on both sides and cooked through. Transfer to the prepared cooling rack and repeat for the rest of the fritters, adding more oil to the skillet as needed.
6. Serve warm with the avocado-jalapeño dipping sauce.

SERVES 4-6 | PREP TIME: 10 MINUTES, PLUS SITTING TIME COOK TIME: 40 MINUTES

Perfect Herb-Roasted Potatoes

Lexi: There are a million ways to prepare a potato, but sometimes, simple is best, and here is our method for making the best oven-roasted potatoes. We start by rinsing the potatoes to remove excess starch, then coat them in a spiced herb mixture for plenty of flavor. The secret ingredient is a bit of cornstarch for a perfectly crispy, browned exterior and a light, fluffy interior. It's our go-to easy side dish for just about any weeknight dinner. Try them with our Citrus-Herb Chicken Kebabs (page 131) and our Greek Chickpea Salad (page 112) for my idea of the perfect balanced dinner!

3lb (1.35kg) unpeeled Yukon gold potatoes, diced into ½-inch (1cm) cubes
3 tbsp olive oil
1½ tbsp cornstarch
2 tsp kosher salt
1 tsp sweet paprika
1 tsp dried oregano
1 tsp dried basil
¾ tsp garlic powder
¾ tsp onion powder
½ tsp dried thyme
½ tsp ground pepper
3 tbsp finely chopped parsley

1. To a large bowl, add the diced potatoes and cover with cold water. Let the potatoes soak for 1 hour to remove excess starch, then drain and rinse with cold water. Transfer the potatoes to a clean tea towel and pat completely dry.
2. Preheat the oven to 400°F (200°C) and line a large sheet pan with parchment paper.
3. To a large bowl, add the potatoes and olive oil and toss to coat. In a small bowl, stir together the cornstarch, salt, paprika, oregano, basil, garlic powder, onion powder, thyme, and pepper. Sprinkle over the potatoes and toss until evenly coated.
4. Spread the potatoes in an even layer on the prepared sheet pan. Roast for 40 to 50 minutes, stirring every 15 minutes, until the potatoes are golden brown and crispy on the exterior and fork tender on the interior. About 10 minutes before the potatoes are done cooking, sprinkle with the parsley, stir, and continue roasting until they're finished cooking. Serve hot.

SERVES 6–8 | PREP TIME: 5 MINUTES COOK TIME: 12 MINUTES

Miso Butter Mushrooms

Earthy, savory, and umami-rich Miso Butter Mushrooms is a side dish that punches well above its weight. They're easy to make but taste like something you would get at a restaurant. You can pair them with just about any protein, like roasted chicken or tofu, but they're particularly good atop a perfectly seared steak. We use a mixture of easy-to-find button or cremini mushrooms and shiitakes, which pack a bit more flavor. Take things to the next level by adding in your favorite wild mushrooms—maitake, oyster, chanterelle, and beech mushrooms are all great choices.

4 tbsp unsalted butter, softened
2 tbsp mild white miso paste
¼ tsp ground black pepper, plus more to taste
2lb (900g) mixed mushrooms, sliced (button, cremini, shitake, etc.)
1½ tsp tamari (or soy sauce if not making gluten-free)
1½ tsp rice vinegar
3 garlic cloves, minced
3 tbsp chopped parsley

1. Using a fork, in a small bowl, mash the butter, then stir in the miso paste and pepper until evenly incorporated. Set aside.
2. To a large skillet over high heat, add the mushrooms and cook for about 5 minutes, stirring occasionally, until the mushrooms have softened and any excess moisture has evaporated.
3. Add the miso butter and stir until melted. Add the tamari and vinegar and cook for 4 to 5 minutes, stirring occasionally, until the mushrooms are browned around the edges.
4. Add the garlic and parsley and cook for 2 minutes, stirring occasionally, until the garlic is softened and fragrant. Serve hot.

SERVES 4–6 | PREP TIME: 35 MINUTES COOK TIME: 25 MINUTES

V

Panko-Crusted Butternut Squash Fries

with Garlic-Parmesan Sauce

Picky kids (and adults!) might be more likely to try a new vegetable if it's in fry form, and honestly, we get it. But instead of deep frying in oil, these "fries" are oven-baked and equally crispy. Any breadcrumbs will work, but panko breadcrumbs make a crunchier coating. If you're dealing with some really picky eaters, you can skip some of the seasonings in the breading and serve the fries up with ketchup instead. But for everyone else, the garlicky, cheesy mayo dipping sauce is a must. Pro tip: When picking out butternut squash, look for ones that have longer "necks" so you can easily cut the flesh into fry-shaped pieces.

FOR THE FRIES

½ cup all-purpose flour
2 tsp kosher salt, divided
½ tsp ground black pepper, divided
½ tsp garlic powder, divided
½ tsp onion powder, divided
3 large eggs
3 tbsp whole milk
1 cup panko breadcrumbs
⅓ cup grated Parmesan
1 tbsp Italian seasoning blend
2¼lb (1kg) butternut squash, peeled and cut into 4 x ½-inch (10 x 1cm) fries
Avocado oil or other cooking spray

FOR THE GARLIC-PARMESAN DIPPING SAUCE

6 tbsp mayonnaise
3 tbsp grated Parmesan
2 tbsp whole milk
1 tbsp Dijon mustard
2 tsp freshly squeezed lemon juice
½ tsp garlic powder
¼ tsp kosher salt
⅛ tsp ground black pepper

1. Preheat the oven to 375°F (190°C) and line a large, rimmed sheet pan with parchment paper.
2. To make the fries, set up three shallow bowls, each about 8 inches (20cm) wide. In the first bowl, whisk together the flour, ½ teaspoon of the salt, ¼ teaspoon of the black pepper, ¼ teaspoon of the garlic powder, and ¼ teaspoon of the onion powder. In the second bowl, whisk together the eggs and milk. In the third bowl, whisk together the panko breadcrumbs, Parmesan, Italian seasoning, and the remaining salt, black pepper, garlic powder, and onion powder.
3. Using one hand and working one fry at a time, coat the fry in the flour mixture, tapping off any excess flour. With the other hand, dip the fry into the egg mixture, letting any excess egg drip off. Lastly, place the fry in the breading mixture and, using your dry hand, evenly coat with the breadcrumbs, pressing lightly to adhere the breadcrumbs in an even layer. Transfer to the prepared sheet pan. Repeat with the remaining squash fries, arranging them on the pan so they're not touching.
4. Spray the squash fries lightly with the cooking spray. Bake for 15 minutes, then carefully flip the fries over one at a time and spray once more with the cooking spray. Bake for another 10 minutes, until crispy and golden brown. Set aside to cool slightly on the sheet pan.
5. To make the dipping sauce, in a small bowl, whisk together the mayonnaise, Parmesan, milk, Dijon mustard, lemon juice, garlic powder, salt, and pepper until smooth.
6. Transfer the fries to a serving plate and serve warm with the dipping sauce on the side.

SERVES 4 | **PREP TIME:** 10 MINUTES **COOK TIME:** 40 MINUTES

Parmesan-Crusted Brussels Sprouts

Lexi: If you've followed any food account on social media recently, you've probably seen some variation of Parmesan-crusted vegetables. I'll be honest, I thought it was a bit of a gimmick at first, but when you really think about it, what can't be improved with a crispy Parmesan crust? Especially, as it turns out, the most polarizing vegetable: brussels sprouts. These have made an appearance at our Thanksgiving table for several years in a row now, and they're kind of a specialty of my husband, Brent. The key is to parcook and heavily season the brussels sprouts so they're almost ready to go once you place them down on a bed of Parmesan. The Parmesan crisps up quickly, so keep an eye on your oven. And don't skip the hot honey-mustard sauce for dipping—it's the best part!

FOR THE BRUSSELS SPROUTS

15 large brussels sprouts
1 tbsp olive oil
1 tsp kosher salt
¼ tsp onion powder
¼ tsp garlic powder
¼ tsp sweet paprika
¼ tsp mustard powder
Pinch of cayenne pepper
1¼ cups finely shredded Parmesan

FOR THE HOT HONEY-MUSTARD SAUCE

¼ cup mayonnaise
2 tbsp Dijon mustard
1 tbsp hot sauce
1 tbsp honey

1. Preheat the oven to 400°F (200°C).
2. To make the brussels sprouts, in a large bowl, toss the brussels sprouts with the olive oil and transfer to a large sheet pan. Cover with aluminum foil and roast for 25 to 30 minutes, stirring halfway through, until fork tender. Remove from the oven and let cool slightly.
3. In a small bowl, combine the salt, onion powder, garlic powder, paprika, mustard powder, and cayenne pepper.
4. Trim the ends off the cooled brussels sprouts and cut them in half lengthwise. Season the cut sides of each sprout with some of the seasoning mix.
5. On another nonstick sheet pan, evenly space about 1 teaspoon of the Parmesan for each halved brussels sprout. Place the sprouts cut-side down on the Parmesan and press gently. Sprinkle the remaining seasoning mix on top of the sprouts.
6. Bake for 10 to 12 minutes, until the Parmesan is golden and crispy. Remove from the oven and let cool slightly.
7. Meanwhile, to make the sauce, in a small bowl, whisk together the mayonnaise, Dijon mustard, hot sauce, and honey until smooth.
8. Using a thin spatula, remove the cooled roasted brussels sprouts from the pan. They should come right off. Serve warm with the hot honey-mustard sauce.

SERVES 4-6 | **PREP TIME:** 10 MINUTES **COOK TIME:** 30 MINUTES

GF V

Harissa-Roasted Carrots

with Tahini-Yogurt Sauce

Roasted carrots don't have to be boring. Harissa, a spicy, warming North African chili seasoning blend, is the perfect complement to sweet, earthy carrots. You should be able to find harissa at most grocery stores, but keep in mind that it's typically available as both a paste and a dry seasoning blend—we're using the latter here. A creamy, lemony tahini-yogurt sauce tones down the spice, and sometimes we also like to serve these up on a bed of creamy hummus. (Try our Loaded Greek Salad Hummus recipe on page 54). You can keep the carrots whole if they're on the smaller side or cut larger pieces on a bias (i.e., diagonal) if you'd rather have bite-size pieces.

FOR THE CARROTS

3 tbsp olive or avocado oil
1 tbsp harissa seasoning
2 tsp honey
1½ tsp lemon zest
1½ tsp dried oregano
1½ tsp kosher salt
½ tsp ground cumin
½ tsp garlic powder
2lb (900g) peeled whole carrots, tops trimmed or removed

FOR THE YOGURT-TAHINI SAUCE

3 tbsp tahini
2 tbsp plain yogurt
1 tbsp freshly squeezed lemon juice
1 tbsp olive oil
1 tsp honey
½ tsp kosher salt
½ tsp garlic powder
¼ tsp ground cumin
Pinch of cayenne pepper

FOR SERVING

¼ cup crumbled feta cheese
2 tbsp pomegranate arils
1 tbsp chopped cilantro (optional)

1. Preheat the oven to 400°F (200°C). Line a sheet pan with parchment paper.
2. In a large bowl, whisk together the olive oil, harissa, honey, lemon zest, oregano, salt, cumin, and garlic powder. Add the carrots and toss well, using tongs or your hands, until the carrots are evenly coated. Transfer the carrots to the sheet pan and spread them into an even layer.
3. Roast for 25 to 30 minutes, stirring halfway through, until fork tender and lightly charred.
4. Meanwhile, to make the sauce, in a medium bowl, whisk together 2 tablespoons of warm water with the tahini, yogurt, lemon juice, olive oil, honey, salt, garlic powder, cumin, and cayenne pepper until no streaks remain. If needed to reach a pourable consistency, add another 1 tablespoon of warm water.
5. When the carrots are finished, remove from the oven and let cool on the sheet pan for a few minutes before transferring to a serving platter. Drizzle with the tahini-yogurt sauce, then top with the feta, pomegranate arils, and cilantro (if using). Serve warm.

SERVES 6 | **PREP TIME:** 20 MINUTES **COOK TIME:** 20 MINUTES

Pan-Fried Shredded Brussels Sprouts

Shredding brussels sprouts completely changes the experience of eating them. Instead of biting through dense layers of leaves, you're left with a light, airy green that's perfect in salads (like our Shaved Brussels Sprout Salad on page 118) or pan-fried with pancetta and shallots, like in this recipe. It's a great way to guarantee that your guests will actually *enjoy* eating brussels sprouts at your next holiday gathering.

- 1 tbsp olive oil
- 4oz (115g) diced pancetta
- ⅔ cup thinly sliced shallot
- 1 tbsp balsamic vinegar
- 1½ tsp finely chopped thyme
- 2 garlic cloves, minced
- 1lb (450g) brussels sprouts, trimmed and shredded (see note)
- ¾ tsp kosher salt
- ¼ tsp ground black pepper
- 2 tbsp finely chopped parsley
- ⅓ cup crumbled goat cheese, to serve
- ¼ cup chopped toasted pecans, to serve
- Pomegranate arils, to serve (optional)

1. Line a plate with a paper towel. To a large skillet over medium heat, add the olive oil and pancetta and cook for 5 minutes, stirring occasionally, until crispy. Using a slotted spoon, transfer the pancetta to the prepared plate, leaving the rendered fat in the skillet. Set aside.
2. To the same skillet, add the shallots, balsamic vinegar, and thyme. Cook for 5 minutes, stirring often, until the shallots soften. Stir in the garlic and cook for 1 minute, stirring often, until fragrant.
3. Add the shredded brussels sprouts, salt, and pepper, mixing well, and cook for 5 to 8 minutes, stirring frequently, until the brussels sprouts are softened, browned, and crispy.
4. Stir in the cooked pancetta and the parsley and cook for an additional 2 to 3 minutes, until the pancetta is sizzling, then remove from the heat.
5. Transfer to a bowl or platter and top with the goat cheese, pecans, and pomegranate (if using). Serve warm.

Make it dairy free: Leave out the goat cheese or swap with your favorite plant-based soft cheese alternative.

Note: To shred the brussels sprouts as thinly as possible, use a food processor with a slicing disc set to 1⁄16 inch (1.5mm) thick, or use a mandoline (with extra care) or a knife. You can also look for pre-shredded, bagged brussels sprouts at the grocery store if you prefer.

SERVES 4–6 | **PREP TIME:** 10 MINUTES **COOK TIME:** 15 MINUTES

Buttered Egg Noodles
with Crispy Breadcrumbs

Let us preface this by saying: These are not your average buttered noodles. There's a bit of backstory you need to be aware of before you dive in. Frankenmuth, Michigan, is a tiny town in the middle of the state that attracts three million visitors a year who come from all over for its Bavarian-style architecture and Bronner's, the world's largest Christmas store. No trip to Frankenmuth is complete without a visit to Zehnder's for a family-style dinner of fried chicken, mashed potatoes, cranberry relish, and most importantly, *the* buttered noodles. They're made with egg noodles cooked in their proprietary poultry seasoning blend (the secret ingredient) and doused in the most buttery cracker mixture you can imagine. There's nothing quite like them—you'll just have to try this recipe to believe us!

7 tbsp salted butter, divided
1lb (450g) wide egg noodles
6 cups chicken broth, divided
1½ tsp poultry seasoning
½ tsp ground black pepper
¼ tsp kosher salt, plus more to taste
⅓ cup crushed Ritz crackers
¼ cup chopped parsley

1. In a large skillet over medium heat, melt 4 tablespoons of the butter. Once bubbling, add the egg noodles, 5 cups of the broth, and the poultry seasoning, pepper, and salt. Stir well to ensure there are no dry noodles.
2. Increase the heat to high and bring to a boil. Stir, then reduce the heat to medium and simmer uncovered for 8 to 10 minutes, stirring occasionally, until most of the liquid is absorbed into the pasta.
3. Meanwhile, in a small skillet over medium-low heat, melt 1 tablespoon of the butter. Add the crushed crackers and stir to completely coat. Cook, stirring occasionally, for 3 to 4 minutes, until the crackers are golden brown and fragrant. Remove from the heat and set aside to cool.
4. Pour the remaining 1 cup broth into the skillet with the pasta and add the remaining 2 tablespoons butter and the parsley. Cook for 4 to 5 minutes, stirring occasionally, until the pasta is al dente and the sauce has thickened slightly.
5. Serve hot topped with the crushed crackers.

SERVES 4–6 | **PREP TIME:** 30 MINUTES, PLUS SITTING TIME **COOK TIME:** 30 MINUTES

Pumpkin Ricotta Gnocchi

Gnocchi made with ricotta instead of potatoes is extra light, airy, pillowy, and dare we say . . . even more delicious! It's the perfect project for a chilly Sunday in October, when you're just craving pasta and a good glass of wine. Or try them for an extra impressive holiday side or a special-occasion vegetarian dinner. We boil and then sear the gnocchi in a simple but flavorful thyme, butter, and Parmesan sauce. Give it a try with our Shaved Brussels Sprout Salad (page 118) for the ultimate fall meal. Bonus: Freeze any uncooked gnocchi for later—your future self will thank you! These can go straight from the freezer to boiling water, where they'll cook in about 3 minutes.

FOR THE GNOCCHI

⅔ cup canned pumpkin purée
⅔ cup whole-milk ricotta
2 cups all-purpose flour, plus more to dust
5¾ tsp kosher salt, divided
⅔ cup grated Parmesan
1 large egg, beaten
¼ tsp ground black pepper
¼ tsp ground nutmeg
⅛ tsp ground cinnamon

FOR THE SAUCE

4 tbsp salted butter, divided
1½ tsp finely chopped thyme
2 tbsp grated Parmesan, plus more to garnish
¼ tsp ground black pepper

1. To make the gnocchi, start by draining excess moisture from the pumpkin and ricotta. To do so, fold several sheets of paper towel, then spread the pumpkin purée on top in a thin layer and let sit for 15 minutes to drain. Repeat the same process with the ricotta on separate paper towels.
2. Meanwhile, dust a pastry mat with flour. Line a sheet pan with parchment paper and lightly dust with flour as well.
3. In a large pot, add 5 quarts of water and 5 teaspoons of the salt and bring to a boil.
4. Meanwhile, to a large bowl, add the drained pumpkin and ricotta, Parmesan, egg, the remaining ¾ teaspoon salt, and the pepper, nutmeg, and cinnamon. Whisk until smooth.
5. Add half of the flour and mix. Add the remaining flour and continue mixing until the dough just comes together. The dough should be soft but not sticky. If too sticky, try working a little bit of flour into the dough until it no longer sticks to your fingers. If too crumbly, add a few drops of water to the dough and knead until it comes together, adding a few more drops of water at a time as needed.
6. Transfer the dough to the floured pastry mat and gently knead until a smooth ball forms. Flatten into a circle, then cut into 8 evenly sized wedges.
7. Using your hands, roll a wedge of dough into a log, dusting with extra flour as needed to prevent sticking, until it's about ¾ inch (2cm) in diameter. Using a knife or bench scraper, cut the log into ½-inch (13mm) pieces. Transfer the gnocchi to the floured sheet pan and repeat with the remaining dough.
8. Working in 3 to 4 batches, cook the gnocchi in the simmering water for 2 to 3 minutes, until they float to the surface. Once they float, cook for an additional 30 seconds. With a slotted spoon, remove the gnocchi from the

water and transfer to a colander to drain. Reserve a few tablespoons of the gnocchi cooking water and set aside.

9. To make the sauce, in a large skillet over medium heat, melt 3 tablespoons of the butter. Add the thyme and cook for about 2 minutes, stirring frequently, until the butter smells nutty and the thyme is fragrant.
10. Add the gnocchi to the sauce and cook for 5 to 7 minutes, stirring occasionally, until lightly browned on all sides.
11. Mix in the remaining 1 tablespoon butter, the reserved gnocchi cooking water, and the Parmesan and pepper. Cook for an additional 2 to 3 minutes, stirring once or twice, until the butter and Parmesan have melted and combined into a thin sauce. Remove from the heat and serve right away with more Parmesan on top.

AIX

Cocktails

SERVES 1 | **PREP TIME:** 5 MINUTES

Tart Cherry Old-Fashioned

Michigan produces about 75 percent of the total tart cherry crop in the US. (Traverse City, Michigan, is nicknamed the Cherry Capital of the World!) Tart cherries have recently gone mainstream for their impressive health benefits, but as proud Michiganders, we have to brag that we've been enjoying tart cherry juice for years and always have a bottle in the fridge. It lends itself perfectly to a fun twist on an old-fashioned, with pure maple syrup for a rich, complex cocktail. Orange is traditional, but we find that lime juice is even better. Pour this over a jumbo ice cube, and enjoy on a breezy summer afternoon.

Ice
3fl oz (90ml) 100% tart cherry juice
2fl oz (60ml) bourbon
½fl oz (15ml) freshly squeezed lime juice
½fl oz (15ml) maple syrup
2–3 dashes of cherry bitters (or Angostura bitters)
1 large ice cube, to serve
Cherry, to garnish
Mint sprig, to garnish

1. Place a lowball glass in the freezer to chill.
2. Fill a cocktail shaker halfway with ice and add the tart cherry juice, bourbon, lime juice, maple syrup, and bitters. Shake vigorously for 15 seconds, then strain into the chilled lowball glass over a large ice cube.
3. Garnish with a cherry and a sprig of mint.

SERVES 2 | **PREP TIME:** 15 MINUTES **COOK TIME:** 5 MINUTES

Caramelized Piña Colada on the Rocks

Another way to think of this cocktail: pineapple upside-down cake in a glass. Buttery, brown sugar–caramelized pineapple is blended with rum, extra pineapple juice, coconut milk, and lime juice for a dangerously delicious sip. Seriously, you'll have to really remind yourself that this drink contains alcohol. As a bonus, the caramelized pineapple is delicious enough to eat on its own, ideally spooned over vanilla ice cream.

2 tbsp salted butter
¼ cup light brown sugar, packed
2 tbsp honey
1 cup diced fresh or frozen pineapple
4fl oz (120ml) white rum
3fl oz (90ml) pineapple juice
2fl oz (60ml) full-fat coconut milk
1fl oz (30ml) freshly squeezed lime juice
Ice
Maraschino cherries, to serve

1. In a medium skillet over medium heat, melt the butter. Stir in the brown sugar and honey. Once the mixture starts to bubble, add in the pineapple. Reduce the heat to medium-low and cook for about 5 minutes, stirring occasionally, until the mixture starts to get very bubbly and foamy.
2. Remove from the heat and transfer to a bowl to cool for about 10 minutes.
3. In a blender, combine the cooled pineapple mixture, rum, pineapple juice, coconut milk, and lime juice and blend until no pineapple pieces remain.
4. Fill a cocktail shaker halfway with ice and add the blended pineapple mixture. Shake well for 15 seconds, then strain the cocktail into 2 highball glasses filled with ice. Serve with a maraschino cherry on each glass.

Make it plant-based: Use a nondairy butter to cook the pineapple and agave instead of honey.

SERVES 1 | **PREP TIME:** 10 MINUTES

Bunny Mary

The Bloody Mary is probably the most polarizing cocktail out there—you either love 'em or you hate 'em. But if you do love a good Bloody Mary, you'll probably also be a big fan of this carrot version! It's made with all the same flavor-boosting ingredients, like pickle juice, horseradish, Tabasco sauce, and Worcestershire sauce, but the base is carrot juice instead of tomato. It's more earthy and less acidic than a traditional Bloody Mary but still has that familiar sweetness. If you're not totally sold, try combining carrot and tomato juice as a starting point. (By the way, there's no better occasion for this cocktail than Easter morning. Just saying.)

FOR ASSEMBLY

2 tsp kosher salt
1 tsp Old Bay seasoning
Lime wedge
Ice
Garnishes of choice (pickles, celery, fresh dill, etc.)

FOR THE COCKTAIL

Ice
4fl oz (120ml) carrot juice
1½fl oz (45ml) vodka
½fl oz (15ml) dill pickle brine
½fl oz (15ml) freshly squeezed lime juice
½ tsp prepared horseradish
2 dashes of Tabasco sauce
2 dashes of gluten-free, plant-based Worcestershire sauce (or regular if no dietary restrictions)
¼ tsp Old Bay seasoning
¼ tsp sweet paprika
¼ tsp ground black pepper
¼ tsp kosher salt

1. In a small bowl, stir together the salt and Old Bay seasoning, then pour the mixture onto a small plate.
2. With a lime wedge, moisten the rim of a highball glass, then coat in the rimming salt and fill the glass with ice.
3. Fill a cocktail shaker halfway with ice, then add the carrot juice, vodka, pickle brine, lime juice, horseradish, Tabasco sauce, Worcestershire sauce, Old Bay seasoning, paprika, black pepper, and salt and shake for 15 seconds.
4. Strain into the prepared glass, and top with your desired garnishes.

SERVES 1 | PREP TIME: 10 MINUTES, PLUS INFUSING TIME COOK TIME: 4 MINUTES

Blueberry, Lemon, and Lavender Gin Cocktail

If you like a fruity, floral, herbal cocktail (or if you're hosting a garden party), this is the one for you. Blueberry juice is sweet and mellow in flavor, which really lets the gin and lavender shine through. Lemon juice adds a punch of much-needed acidity to brighten everything up. Make sure to use culinary-grade lavender in the syrup. It's grown specifically for its aroma and flavor, whereas the lavender in your garden is just not going to taste the same. If you're not big on lavender, this is also delicious with a splash of elderflower liqueur instead.

FOR THE LAVENDER SIMPLE SYRUP

½ cup granulated sugar

2 tsp dried culinary-grade lavender

FOR THE COCKTAIL

Ice

3fl oz (90ml) blueberry juice

2fl oz (60ml) gin

¾fl oz (22ml) freshly squeezed lemon juice

Lavender sprigs, to garnish (optional)

Fresh blueberries, to garnish

1. To make the simple syrup, in a small saucepan over medium heat, combine the sugar, lavender, and ½ cup of water and cook, stirring, until the sugar is completely dissolved. Bring to a boil and cook for 1 minute, then reduce the heat to low and simmer for an additional 3 minutes. Remove from the heat and let the syrup infuse for 30 minutes before straining through a fine-mesh sieve.
2. To make the cocktail, fill a cocktail shaker halfway with ice, then add the blueberry juice, gin, 1 ounce (30ml) of the lavender simple syrup, and the lemon juice. Shake for 15 seconds, then pour into a glass partially filled with ice.
3. Garnish with a lavender sprig (if using) and a few fresh blueberries.

Note: This recipe makes enough lavender simple syrup for 8 cocktails. Store the extra in an airtight container in the refrigerator for several weeks.

SERVES 6 | **PREP TIME:** 40 MINUTES **COOK TIME:** 5 MINUTES

Rosé Lemonade

A few years ago, we took a post-COVID family trip to the south of France, where we spent a week in an idyllic countryside home with several of our former exchange students and their families. It was one of the best weeks we've ever had, and it was spent eating, exploring, and mostly sitting by the pool with a glass of rosé lemonade. This is truly the ideal poolside summer cocktail—it's refreshing, light, slightly bubbly, and almost a bit *too* easy to sip on. For an extra effervescent drink, use sparkling rosé.

FOR THE LEMONADE MIXTURE

6 tbsp granulated sugar
1 tbsp lemon zest
½ cup freshly squeezed lemon juice

FOR THE COCKTAIL

One 750ml bottle good quality rosé wine, chilled
¾ cup sparkling water or club soda, chilled
6 lavender sprigs, to garnish

1. To make the lemonade mixture, in a small bowl, combine the sugar and lemon zest. Massage the lemon zest into the sugar for about 1 minute to release the oils in the zest.
2. In a medium saucepan over medium heat, combine the sugar-zest mixture with the lemon juice and ¼ cup of water. Cook for 5 to 8 minutes, stirring frequently, until the sugar is dissolved, then remove from the heat and let cool to room temperature.
3. Once cooled, strain the lemonade mixture through a fine-mesh sieve to remove the zest.
4. To make the cocktail, in a large pitcher, combine the strained lemonade mixture with the chilled rosé and sparkling water, and stir.
5. Divide the cocktail between 6 glasses and garnish each with a sprig of lavender.

Note: Make the lemonade mixture ahead of time and keep it chilled in the refrigerator for up to 1 week.

SERVES 6 | **PREP TIME:** 10 MINUTES, PLUS INFUSING TIME **COOK TIME:** 5 MINUTES

Spicy Peach-Blackberry Margarita

During the summer months, we like to keep a batch of jalapeño simple syrup in the fridge at all times. You never know when you might need a last-minute margarita on a Friday night, and it's our favorite easy way to pack in lots of flavor without much effort. (Plus, if you're growing jalapeños in your garden, you probably need as many jalapeño recipes as possible!) The spicy syrup perfectly balances out the sweetness of fresh peaches and blackberries in this refreshing, vibrant margarita that truly tastes like summer in a glass. A splash of club soda isn't traditional, but a bit of fizz brightens everything up. For an extra-spicy cocktail, try infusing your tequila with jalapeño overnight (see page 262).

FOR THE JALAPEÑO SIMPLE SYRUP

⅔ cup granulated sugar
1 medium jalapeño, sliced into rounds

FOR THE PEACH PURÉE

2 cups diced peaches

FOR EACH COCKTAIL

3 large blackberries, plus more to garnish
Ice
1½fl oz (45ml) reposado tequila
¾fl oz (22ml) freshly squeezed lime juice
½fl oz (15ml) orange liqueur (Cointreau, Grand Marnier, or other triple sec brand)
1fl oz (30ml) club soda
Peach slices, to garnish

1. To make the simple syrup, in a small saucepan over medium-high heat, combine ⅔ cup of water, the sugar, and jalapeño. Cook, stirring until the sugar dissolves, then bring to a boil and let cook for 2 minutes. Reduce the heat to low and let simmer for another 3 minutes, then remove from the heat. Let the syrup infuse for 30 minutes before straining through a fine-mesh sieve to remove the jalapeño. Let cool completely before using. (See notes.)
2. To make the peach purée, to a blender, add the peaches and blend until smooth. Strain through a fine-mesh sieve to remove any pulp. (See notes.)
3. To make the cocktails, in each cocktail glass, add the blackberries and muddle until completely crushed, then fill the glass with ice. Fill a cocktail shaker halfway with ice, add 2 ounces (60ml) of the peach purée, ¾ ounce (22ml) of the jalapeño simple syrup, and the tequila, lime juice, and orange liqueur. Shake for 15 seconds, then strain into the cocktail glass and top off with the club soda.
4. Stir gently to incorporate the muddled blackberries and garnish with a peach slice and blackberry before serving.

Notes: Makes enough jalapeño simple syrup for 8 to 10 cocktails. Store extra in an airtight container in the refrigerator for up to several weeks.

Makes enough peach purée for 8 cocktails. Store extra in an airtight container in the refrigerator for 2 to 3 days.

SERVES 4 | PREP TIME: 10 MINUTES, PLUS FREEZING TIME

Frozen Strawberry-Watermelon Daiquiri

If you associate a frozen daiquiri with an artificially colored, sugary slushie that gets pumped out of a machine, we're here to tell you that it doesn't have to be that way. In fact, it should never be that way, because a real daiquiri is one of the most refreshing, delicious cocktails out there! Our version combines frozen watermelon and strawberries with rum, freshly squeezed lime juice, and just a touch of sugar. It's fruit-forward, cooling, and fresh, and there's nothing better on a steamy summer day.

1 cup diced watermelon
1 cup diced frozen strawberries
6fl oz (180ml) white rum
2fl oz (60ml) freshly squeezed lime juice
2fl oz (60ml) simple syrup
Fresh mint, to garnish

1. Line a sheet pan with parchment paper. On the sheet pan, spread the watermelon into a single layer. Transfer to the freezer for about 3 hours, until frozen solid.
2. In a high-speed blender, combine the frozen watermelon, frozen strawberries, white rum, lime juice, and simple syrup and blend until completely smooth.
3. Pour into four glasses and garnish each with a sprig of mint.

Sangria Sorbet

It couldn't be any easier to blend up a batch of this sangria sorbet, and it's the perfect boozy treat for a hot summer day! The alcohol prevents the fruit from freezing solid, so it's always easy to scoop, even straight from the freezer. If you don't want to wait for it to freeze, you can also serve it up slushie-style. It's easy to change up the recipe with various fruits, but our favorite combination (pictured here) is strawberries, peaches, and raspberries for a vibrant, tart, perfectly sweet sorbet. And no—you don't need an ice cream machine to give this a try.

1¼lb (550g) mixed frozen fruit, thawed at room temperature for 15 minutes
2 cups (480ml) dry white wine (sauvignon blanc, pinot grigio, chardonnay, etc.)
⅓ cup honey
1fl oz (30ml) orange liqueur (Cointreau, Grand Marnier, or other triple sec brand)
1fl oz (30ml) freshly squeezed lemon juice

1. In a blender, combine the frozen fruit, wine, honey, orange liqueur, and lemon juice and blend for 1 minute, until completely smooth.
2. Pour the frozen mixture into a shallow, freezer-safe medium container (about 9 x 5 inches / 23 x 12cm) and transfer to the freezer for at least 6 hours, until solid. Scoop and enjoy right away.

Storage instructions: Store in a sealed container in the freezer for up to 3 months.

SERVES 2 | PREP TIME: 10 MINUTES, PLUS FREEZING TIME

Frozen Bourbon Arnold Palmer

Lexi: If you're anything like my dad, your idea of a perfect summer day might have something to do with playing golf, watching golf, or thinking about golf while you sip on a Frozen Bourbon Arnold Palmer. (If you're lost, the drink—iced tea and lemonade—was named after its creator, Arnold Palmer, a famous professional golfer from the 1960s.) Of course, it's perfect for any scorching summer day, no matter your golf preferences. You can't go wrong with the combination of freshly brewed black tea, lemon, honey, and bourbon, frozen into ice cubes and blended up into a cooling, satisfying slushie.

- 1 sachet of black tea (like English Breakfast)
- 8fl oz (240ml) hot water
- 2fl oz (60ml) freshly squeezed lemon juice
- 2fl oz (60ml) honey
- 4fl oz (120ml) bourbon
- 1½ cups crushed ice
- Mint sprigs, to garnish

1. In a large measuring cup with a spout, add the tea bag and hot water and let steep for about 4 minutes, until brewed to your liking. Remove the tea bag, then whisk in the lemon juice and honey until the honey is fully dissolved. Let cool to room temperature.
2. Pour the lemonade-tea mixture into ice cube trays, then transfer to the freezer for about 4 hours, until frozen solid.
3. Once frozen, in a blender, combine the tea ice cubes with the bourbon and the crushed ice. Blend on high speed until smooth.
4. Divide the mixture between 2 highball, Collins, or old-fashioned glasses, garnish with a sprig of mint, and serve right away.

Note: To make this into a mocktail, simply leave out the bourbon and add 4 ounces (120ml) chilled black tea when blending.

SERVES 1 | **PREP TIME: 2 HOURS**

Grape-arita

Grape juice isn't just for lunchboxes. It makes for a surprisingly delicious, sweet, and tart margarita too! Make sure to use 100 percent concord grape juice (not from concentrate)—or even better, if concord grapes are in season, make the juice yourself. Add several cups of fresh concord grapes to a saucepan over medium heat, and smash them with a potato masher to extract the juice. Let the mixture simmer gently for about 10 minutes, mash again, then strain the mixture through a fine-mesh sieve and let the juice cool completely before using. The sugared grapes we make for garnish are so much fun to eat, but they're completely optional.

FOR THE SUGARED GRAPES

6 tbsp sugar, divided
¾ cup concord or white grapes

FOR THE COCKTAIL

Ice
2fl oz (60ml) unsweetened pure concord grape juice
1½fl oz (45ml) reposado tequila
½fl oz (15ml) orange liqueur (Cointreau, Grand Marnier, or other triple sec brand)
½fl oz (15ml) freshly squeezed lime juice
½fl oz (15ml) agave nectar

1. To make the sugared grapes, in a small saucepan over medium heat, combine 3 tablespoons of the sugar and 2 tablespoons water. Bring to a low boil, stirring constantly, until the sugar is completely dissolved. Remove from the heat and let cool to room temperature.
2. Once cooled, add the grapes to the syrup and stir to coat. Using a slotted spoon, transfer the grapes to a cooling rack set over a sheet pan. Let sit for about 1 hour.
3. On a small plate, spread the remaining 3 tablespoons sugar. Roll the cooled grapes, one or two at a time, in the sugar to coat. On a clean rack, place the coated grapes to dry for 1 to 2 hours. (See note.)
4. To make the cocktail, fill a cocktail shaker halfway with ice and add the grape juice, tequila, orange liqueur, lime juice, and agave. Shake vigorously for 15 seconds. Strain into a glass filled with ice. Garnish with 2 to 3 sugared grapes skewered on a cocktail pick and serve.

Note: Makes enough sugared grapes for 6 to 8 cocktails. Store extra in the refrigerator for up to 1 week.

SERVES 1 | PREP TIME: 5 MINUTES

Apple Cider Dark 'n' Stormy

Lexi: A Dark 'n' Stormy is one of my husband's favorite cocktail orders, specifically with extra-dark rum and spicy ginger beer. Apple cider is the perfect addition when it's in season, especially if you swap out regular simple syrup for a splash of pure maple syrup. It's crisp, refreshing, spiced, and even better, just as easy to make as it is to drink.

Ice
2fl oz (60ml) dark rum
2fl oz (60ml) fresh apple cider
½fl oz (15ml) freshly squeezed lime juice
½fl oz (15ml) maple syrup
1fl oz (30ml) ginger beer

1. In a cocktail shaker filled halfway with ice, combine the rum, apple cider, lime juice, and maple syrup.
2. Shake vigorously for 15 seconds, then strain into a highball glass filled with ice. Top with the ginger beer and stir gently before enjoying.

SERVES 2 | **PREP TIME:** 10 MINUTES, PLUS INFUSING TIME **COOK TIME:** 7 MINUTES

Pumpkin Smash

We know what you're thinking: Pumpkin spice doesn't belong in a cocktail. It might sound basic, but it's unexpectedly delicious, especially paired with freshly squeezed orange juice! We tested this recipe with several types of liquor—gin, bourbon, and even tequila—but vodka won out. It's smooth, a little fruity, and pleasantly spiced, thanks to the cinnamon, ginger, cloves, and vanilla bean. You'll want to make double of the pumpkin spice syrup to use in lattes or for drizzling over pancakes, waffles, or yogurt. We promise, homemade is *so* much better than the super sugary, artificially flavored stuff you get at you-know-which coffee joint.

FOR THE PUMPKIN SPICE SIMPLE SYRUP

½ cup maple syrup
¼ cup pumpkin purée
½ a vanilla bean, about 5 inches (12cm) long
2 cinnamon sticks
½ tbsp minced ginger
15 cloves

FOR THE COCKTAILS

Ice
3fl oz (90ml) vodka
2fl oz (60ml) freshly squeezed orange juice
1fl oz (30ml) orange liqueur (Cointreau, Grand Marnier, or other triple sec brand)
1fl oz (30ml) freshly squeezed lime juice
2fl oz (60ml) club soda

1. To make the simple syrup, in a saucepan over medium-low heat, combine ½ cup of water and the maple syrup and pumpkin purée. Whisk to combine.
2. With a small paring knife, cut a lengthwise slit from the top of the vanilla bean pod to the bottom. Using the edge of the knife, scrape the seeds from the pod and add directly to the saucepan, along with the scraped pod and the cinnamon sticks, ginger, and cloves. Increase the heat to medium-high and bring to a boil, then reduce the heat to medium-low and let simmer for 5 to 7 minutes, stirring occasionally, until fragrant.
3. Remove the saucepan from the heat and let the syrup infuse for 30 minutes. Strain through a fine-mesh sieve, then let cool completely before using. (See note.)
4. To make the cocktails, fill a cocktail shaker halfway with ice, then add the vodka, orange juice, orange liqueur, lime juice, and 2 ounces (60ml) of the pumpkin spice simple syrup. Shake vigorously for 15 seconds. Strain evenly between 2 glasses filled with ice. Top each glass with 1 ounce (30ml) of the club soda and stir before serving.

Note: Makes enough pumpkin-spice simple syrup for 5 cocktails. Store extra in an airtight container in the refrigerator for up to several weeks.

SERVES 1 | **PREP TIME: 5 MINUTES**

Cranberry-Orange Whiskey Cocktail

We've made this cocktail every Christmas or Thanksgiving (and sometimes both) for the last several years to rave reviews from our friends and family. It's a perfectly balanced drink that brings together all the best holiday flavors! If you're not a whiskey drinker, it's equally delicious with vodka for a milder, more refreshing sip. If you prefer to make a big batch in a pitcher, be sure to stir it well before serving, and wait to add the ginger beer and ice until just before enjoying.

Ice
3fl oz (90ml) freshly squeezed orange juice
2fl oz (60ml) whiskey
1fl oz (30ml) no-sugar-added cranberry juice
½fl oz (15ml) orange liqueur (Cointreau or other triple sec brand)
½fl oz (15ml) freshly squeezed lemon juice
½fl oz (15ml) simple syrup
2 sprigs fresh thyme, plus more to garnish (optional)
1 large ice cube, to serve
2fl oz (60ml) ginger beer
Orange peel, to garnish (optional)

1. In a cocktail shaker filled halfway with ice, combine the orange juice, whiskey, cranberry juice, orange liqueur, lemon juice, simple syrup, and thyme. Shake vigorously for 15 seconds, then strain into a chilled glass with a large ice cube.
2. Top off with the ginger beer and garnish with the orange peel and more thyme (if using).

SERVES 2 | PREP TIME: 15 MINUTES

Tiramisu Martini

Lexi: This luxurious, decadent martini is tiramisu in liquid form, and I really can't think of a better after-dinner drink. The base is essentially an espresso martini (so you should probably avoid this recipe if you're caffeine sensitive), it's topped with a whipped mascarpone layer for plenty of rich, creamy flavor in every sip. For a true tiramisu experience, don't skip the dusting of cocoa powder and the ladyfinger for dipping. Cin cin (cheers)!

¼ cup heavy cream, plus more as needed
2 tbsp mascarpone cheese
2 tsp powdered sugar
1 tsp vanilla extract
Ice
3fl oz (90ml) vodka
2fl oz (60ml) freshly brewed espresso, cooled to room temperature
2fl oz (60ml) coffee liqueur (like Kahlúa)
Cocoa powder, to garnish
2 ladyfinger cookies, to serve

1. Place 2 martini glasses in the freezer to chill for 10 minutes while you make the cocktail.
2. In a small bowl, whisk together the heavy cream, mascarpone, powdered sugar, and vanilla extract until smooth and reaches a light, pourable consistency. If too thick, add an additional ½ teaspoon heavy cream. Set aside.
3. In a cocktail shaker filled halfway with ice, combine the vodka, espresso, and coffee liqueur. Shake vigorously for 10 to 15 seconds, then strain into the chilled martini glasses.
4. Spoon the mascarpone mixture over the martinis and lightly dust with the cocoa powder. Serve with a ladyfinger.

SERVES 2 | PREP TIME: 10 MINUTES

Blood Orange Pisco Sour

Lexi: Our family hosted eight exchange students during my childhood, and each of them lived with us for about a year and became part of our family. I'm still very close with several of my "sisters" to this day. A few years ago, we visited Cata, our former Chilean exchange student. On our way there, we stopped in Peru, where we had (and loved!) our very first pisco sour, but it wasn't until we arrived in Chile that we discovered the pisco sour is a hotly debated topic between the two countries. We got an earful from Cata on the Chilean perspective, took a tour of a local pisco distillery, and left with a newfound appreciation for the brandy-like spirit. We've continued to drink Chilean piscos at home, and we prefer ours with a foamy egg-white topping, which isn't always traditional. (You can leave it out if preferred.) Freshly squeezed blood orange juice is our favorite citrus of choice, but if you can't find any, regular orange or grapefruit juice will do the trick.

1 pasteurized egg white, about 2 tbsp
4fl oz (120ml) pisco
3fl oz (90ml) freshly squeezed blood orange juice
1½fl oz (45ml) freshly squeezed lime juice
1½fl oz (45ml) simple syrup
2 dashes of Angostura bitters
Ice

1. Put 2 cocktail glasses in the freezer to chill.
2. In a cocktail shaker, combine the egg white and pisco. Shake vigorously for 15 seconds and let sit for 10 minutes.
3. Add the blood orange juice, lime juice, simple syrup, and bitters. Add a handful of ice and shake well for 30 seconds, then strain into the chilled cocktail glasses. The egg white will settle at the top of the glass, creating a foamy topping.

SERVES 2 | PREP TIME: 10 MINUTES, PLUS COOLING TIME COOK TIME: 5 MINUTES

Red Velvet Martini

This recipe is part cocktail, part dessert, and completely perfect for date night at home (especially Valentine's Day!). It's rich, creamy, and decadent but still sophisticated. The key ingredient is our homemade raspberry-chocolate simple syrup. If you're used to overly sweet restaurant cocktails, you'll be pleasantly surprised by how much of a difference real fruit makes versus the artificially flavored syrups from a bottle. The tartness really comes through, and it's balanced out by unsweetened cocoa powder for that rich, velvety flavor you get from a red velvet cake. You'll have extra simple syrup left over to enjoy, and it's the perfect addition to a morning latte.

FOR THE RASPBERRY-CHOCOLATE SIMPLE SYRUP

6oz (175g) fresh or frozen raspberries
½ cup granulated sugar
1 tbsp unsweetened cocoa powder

FOR THE COCKTAIL

Powdered freeze-dried raspberries, to garnish (optional)
Ice
2fl oz (60ml) vodka, chilled
2fl oz (60ml) raspberry liqueur (e.g., Chambord)
2fl oz (60ml) heavy cream, very cold
Raspberries, to garnish
Shaved dark chocolate, to garnish (optional)

1. To make the simple syrup, in a small saucepan over medium heat, combine the raspberries, sugar, and ½ cup of water. Using a wooden spoon, break down the raspberries into a mash. Whisk in the cocoa powder and let simmer for 5 minutes, stirring occasionally, until the raspberries are very soft.
2. Strain the syrup through a fine-mesh sieve into a bowl, pressing as much of the raspberry juice through as possible. Let cool to room temperature for 20 to 30 minutes, or speed it up by placing it in the refrigerator. (See note.)
3. Meanwhile, place 2 martini glasses in the freezer to chill.
4. Just before making the cocktail, remove the glasses from the freezer. If you like, on a small dish, place the powdered raspberries (if using) in a thin layer, rim the glasses in the simple syrup, then dip in the powdered raspberries.
5. To make the cocktail, fill a cocktail shaker halfway with ice. Add the vodka, raspberry liqueur, heavy cream, and 1½ ounces (45ml) of the raspberry-chocolate syrup. Shake for 15 seconds, then strain into the chilled martini glasses.
6. Garnish with a few raspberries and shaved dark chocolate (if using).

Note: Makes enough raspberry-chocolate simple syrup for 6 cocktails. Store extra in an airtight container in the refrigerator for up to several weeks.

SERVES 1 | **PREP TIME:** 5 MINUTES

Pineapple and Passion Fruit Rum Punch

Beth: When the kids were growing up, I used to plan a family lūʻau every February, when it's extra cold and bleak in Michigan. We would crank up the heat in our house, go all out on Hawaiian-themed food and decorations, throw on a summery outfit, and pretend we were somewhere far, far away on a beach. It's such a fun way to break up the dreary winter months, and it would be *extra* fun with a batch of rum punch! Our Pineapple and Passion Fruit Rum Punch is light, tart, and sweet, with a splash of grenadine that gives it a mesmerizing sunset effect. Passion fruit juice can be a little tricky to find depending on where you live. We like to use the Ceres brand, but if you can't find any, just use more pineapple, mango, guava, or orange juice.

Ice
2fl oz (60ml) white rum
1fl oz (30ml) pineapple juice
1fl oz (30ml) passion fruit juice
1fl oz (30ml) mango or guava nectar
1fl oz (30ml) freshly squeezed orange juice
¼fl oz (7ml) freshly squeezed lime juice
½fl oz (15ml) grenadine

1. In a cocktail shaker filled halfway with ice, combine the rum, pineapple juice, passion fruit juice, mango or guava nectar, orange juice, and lime juice. Shake vigorously for 15 seconds, then pour into a glass filled with ice.
2. Slowly pour the grenadine into the glass. It will collect on the bottom, creating a beautiful layered effect. Before drinking, stir the cocktail gently to incorporate.

Desserts

MAKES 36 | PREP TIME: 20 MINUTES COOK TIME: 20 MINUTES

V

Pecan, Cherry, and White Chocolate Cookies

Beth: I am notorious for jazzing up a batch of classic chocolate chip cookies with all sorts of pantry odds and ends. What can I say? I love a maximalist cookie. This is my tried-and-true combination. Chewy, decadent, and packed with toasted coconuts and pecans, plus dried cherries and white chocolate chips, you won't be able to stop at just one of these cookies. They have a little bit of everything! If you can't have nuts, leave out the pecans and add in more coconut. These are also great with semisweet or dark chocolate chips if that's more your style.

¾ cup roughly chopped pecans
¾ cup shredded sweetened coconut
1 cup unsalted butter, softened
¾ cup light brown sugar, packed
¾ cup granulated sugar
2 tsp vanilla extract
2 large eggs
2¼ cups all-purpose flour
1 tsp baking soda
½ tsp kosher salt
½ tsp ground cinnamon
1 cup white chocolate chips
1 cup unsweetened dried cherries, chopped

1. Preheat the oven to 350°F (180°C). Line two sheet pans with parchment paper. If both sheet pans can't fit side by side on the middle rack, position one rack in the middle and one in the bottom third of the oven.
2. To a medium skillet over medium heat, add the pecans. Cook, stirring often, for 3 minutes, until the pecans are fragrant, then add in the coconut and cook for another 3 to 4 minutes, stirring often, until fragrant and lightly toasted. (Keep a close eye on the skillet to prevent burning.) Transfer to a plate and set aside to cool.
3. In a large bowl, combine the butter, brown sugar, and granulated sugar. Using an electric mixer on medium speed, whisk for about 3 minutes, until light and fluffy. Add the vanilla extract, then one egg at a time, mixing between each addition until well incorporated.
4. In a separate bowl, whisk together the flour, baking soda, salt, and cinnamon. Working in 2 to 3 batches, gradually add the flour mixture to the wet mixture, mixing between each addition, until the dough comes together. Stir in the toasted pecans and coconut and the white chocolate chips and dried cherries.
5. Using a 2-tablespoon cookie dough scoop, portion the dough and place the portions on the sheet pans about 2 inches (5cm) apart. Bake for 11 to 13 minutes, until the cookies are lightly golden brown. Allow to cool on the sheet pans for 5 to 6 minutes, then transfer to a cooling rack to cool completely.

SERVES 9–12 | **PREP TIME:** 15 MINUTES, PLUS CHILLING TIME **COOK TIME:** 35 MINUTES

Salted Mango Margarita Bars

Say hello to your favorite cocktail in dessert form! A buttery shortbread crust anchors a tangy citrus-forward filling with just the right amount of fresh mango to mellow out the flavor. The tequila and orange liqueur really come through, so be careful to keep these at the adults-only table. Serve them chilled with a pinch of flaky salt on top for the full margarita effect.

FOR THE CRUST

½ cup salted butter, softened
½ cup granulated sugar
1 tsp vanilla extract
½ tsp kosher salt
1 cup plus 2 tbsp all-purpose flour

FOR THE FILLING

1½ cups diced fresh or frozen and thawed mango
½ cup freshly squeezed lime juice
3 tbsp tequila
2 tbsp orange juice
2 tbsp orange liqueur (e.g., Cointreau)
2 tsp lime zest
2 tsp orange zest
One 14oz (396g) can sweetened condensed milk
6 large egg yolks
¼ tsp kosher salt
Flaky salt, to garnish (optional)

1. Preheat the oven to 350°F (180°C). Line an 8-inch (20cm) square pan with parchment paper.
2. To make the crust, in a large bowl, combine the butter, sugar, vanilla extract, and salt. With a hand mixer, beat on medium speed for 30 seconds, until smooth. Add the flour and mix for about a minute, until a crumbly mixture forms.
3. Press the crust mixture into the bottom of the prepared pan in an even layer. Using a fork, dock the dough all over. Bake for 20 to 22 minutes, until the crust is lightly browned around the edges and is still mostly pale in the center. Set aside.
4. To make the filling, in a blender, combine the mango, lime juice, tequila, orange juice, orange liqueur, lime zest, and orange zest. Blend until completely smooth. If the mango is very fibrous, strain the mixture through a fine-mesh sieve to remove any stringy bits. (This is usually not necessary.)
5. No more than 10 minutes before baking, in a medium bowl, whisk together the condensed milk, egg yolks, and salt until smooth. Whisk in the mango mixture until smooth.
6. Pour the filling over the crust and bake for 15 to 18 minutes, until the curd is set around the edges and slightly jiggly in the center. Let cool completely at room temperature, then transfer to the refrigerator to chill and set for 1 to 2 hours before slicing.
7. Top with flaky salt just before serving (if using).

SERVES 8 | PREP TIME: 10 MINUTES COOK TIME: 35 MINUTES

V

Strawberry-Peach Spoon Cake

Spoon cakes are perfect for summer—they're no fuss, no frills, and a great way to use up the best seasonal fruit. If you've never heard of a spoon cake, they're called that because this cake is so tender, you can eat it with a spoon! The batter comes together with a whisk and a mixing bowl in just a few minutes. Lemon zest goes a long way in adding bright, punchy flavor to the batter, and fresh strawberries and peaches get super jammy both in and on top of the cake. The result is soft, rich, and almost pudding-like. Serve it up with a big spoon (this isn't the kind of cake you can slice), and don't forget the vanilla ice cream!

1 tbsp unsalted butter, for greasing the pan
1 cup all-purpose flour, plus more for dusting the pan
⅔ cup granulated sugar
⅓ cup light brown sugar, packed
2 tsp lemon zest
½ cup vegetable oil
2 large eggs, room temperature
¼ cup whole milk
2 tsp freshly squeezed lemon juice
1 tsp vanilla extract
1 tsp baking powder
½ tsp baking soda
½ tsp ground cinnamon
¼ tsp kosher salt
¾ cup hulled and sliced strawberries
¾ cup sliced peaches
1 tbsp coarse sugar (turbinado, demerara, etc.), for topping

1. Preheat the oven to 350°F (180°C). Grease a square 9-inch (23cm) baking pan with the butter, then lightly cover the bottom and sides of the pan with flour.
2. In a large bowl, combine the granulated sugar, brown sugar, and lemon zest. Using your hands, massage the zest into the sugar for 30 seconds. Whisk in the oil, eggs, milk, lemon juice, and vanilla extract until all the ingredients are combined and no streaks remain.
3. In a separate large bowl, whisk together the 1 cup of flour, baking powder, baking soda, cinnamon, and salt. Add the dry ingredients to the wet ingredients and mix until just combined. Be careful not to overmix!
4. Pour the batter into the prepared baking dish. Arrange the strawberry and peach slices evenly over the top and gently press into the batter (see note). Sprinkle evenly with the coarse sugar.
5. Bake for 32 to 35 minutes, until the top is golden brown and a toothpick inserted into the center comes out clean. Let cool in the pan for 10 to 15 minutes before serving.

Note: To prevent excess moisture in the cake, make sure to pat the sliced strawberries and peaches dry with a paper towel before adding to the cake batter.

SERVES 8–12 | **PREP TIME:** 25 MINUTES, PLUS CHILLING TIME **COOK TIME:** 6 MINUTES

Sweet and Salty Goat Cheese Cheesecake
with Raspberry Coulis

We both love cheesecake but don't love baking it, so we're thrilled to tell you that this recipe is no bake! (What a relief, right?) It's still super fluffy, light, and creamy, and the goat cheese adds just the right amount of tangy flavor without overpowering the cream cheese. Instead of a classic graham cracker crust, this one is made with pretzels and pistachios. Either way, you absolutely cannot skip the coulis, which is just a super simple fruit sauce. We like it best with raspberries, but it's also delicious with blueberries, blackberries, or a blend of berries. To ensure the cheesecake filling is super creamy with no lumps, it's key to let the goat cheese and cream cheese come to room temperature before mixing.

FOR THE PRETZEL-PISTACHIO CRUST

- 1 cup mini salted pretzels
- ½ cup roasted salted pistachios
- ¼ cup granulated sugar
- ½ tsp ground cinnamon
- ½ cup unsalted butter, melted

FOR THE FILLING

- 1 cup heavy cream, cold
- 1lb (450g) goat cheese, softened
- 1lb (450g) cream cheese, softened
- 1½ tbsp freshly squeezed lemon juice
- 1 tbsp lemon zest
- 2 tsp vanilla extract
- 1 cup powdered sugar

FOR THE RASPBERRY COULIS

- 3 tbsp cornstarch
- 12oz (350g) fresh or frozen raspberries, plus more fresh raspberries for topping (optional)
- ¼ cup granulated sugar
- 1½ tbsp freshly squeezed lemon juice
- ½ tsp lemon zest

1. To make the crust, in a food processor, combine the pretzels, pistachios, sugar, and cinnamon and pulse several times, until it reaches the consistency of fine crumbs. Pour in the melted butter and pulse until the mixture comes together. Into a round 9-inch (23 cm) springform pan, press the crust evenly into the bottom. Set aside in the refrigerator while you prepare the filling.
2. To make the filling, to a medium bowl, add the heavy cream. Using a hand mixer on medium speed, beat the cream for about 5 minutes, until medium peaks form that stick up but fold over when the beaters are removed from the cream. Set the whipped cream aside.
3. In a separate large bowl, add the goat cheese and cream cheese. Using a hand mixer on medium speed, beat for 2 to 3 minutes, until light and fluffy. Add the lemon juice, lemon zest, and vanilla extract, then beat in the powdered sugar until well combined.

4. Using a spatula, gently fold the whipped cream into the cheese mixture until no streaks remain. Pour the filling onto the chilled crust. With an offset spatula, spread the filling into an even layer. Cover and refrigerate for at least 5 hours or overnight to set.
5. To make the raspberry coulis, in a small bowl, whisk together ⅓ cup of water and the cornstarch. In a medium saucepan over medium heat, combine the raspberries, cornstarch mixture, sugar, lemon juice, and lemon zest. Cook for 6 to 8 minutes, stirring often and mashing with the back of a spoon, until the berries are completely broken down.
6. Strain the raspberries through a fine-mesh sieve to remove the seeds, pressing as much liquid through as possible. Let the coulis cool completely before topping the cheesecake. Tip: You can make the coulis right after making the cheesecake and keep it in the refrigerator until ready to serve.
7. To serve, pour the coulis over the cheesecake, then top with more fresh raspberries (if using). Using a sharp knife, slice the cake into 8 to 12 pieces and enjoy.

Storage instructions: Store in the refrigerator in an airtight container for up to 5 days.

MAKES 9–12 SQUARES | **PREP TIME:** 10 MINUTES, PLUS COOLING TIME **COOK TIME:** 55 MINUTES

Apricot Squares

Beth: This is one of our oldest and most frequently made family recipes, and I still have my grandma's handwritten version in my recipe box. I grew up making these with my mom and grandma every Christmas, and we always had to make an extra pan just for my dad, or else they would be gone within the hour! This recipe may sound old-fashioned, but they're still a hit among family and friends to this day. Don't let the dried apricots turn you off—the tangy, tart flavor is absolutely delicious paired with a buttery brown sugar–streusel crust and topping. They're also fantastic with dried cherries instead of apricots.

FOR THE APRICOT FILLING

1½ cups light brown sugar, packed
1lb (450g) dried apricots, quartered
1 tsp vanilla extract

FOR THE CRUST AND TOPPING

1½ cups quick-cook oats
1½ cups all-purpose flour
1 cup light brown sugar, packed
1¼ tsp baking soda
½ tsp ground cinnamon
¼ tsp kosher salt
¾ cup unsalted butter, melted

1. Preheat the oven to 350°F (180°C) and line a 9 x 13-inch (23 x 33cm) pan with parchment paper.
2. To make the filling, in a medium saucepan over medium heat, combine 1½ cups of water and the brown sugar and stir until the sugar is dissolved. Bring the mixture to a boil, then add the apricots. Reduce the heat to low and simmer for 20 minutes, stirring occasionally, until the apricots have softened.
3. Remove from the heat and stir in the vanilla extract, then let cool for 20 minutes. Transfer the cooled mixture to a blender and pulse until mostly smooth but with some texture remaining. Be sure to crack the lid away from you to prevent heat-related pressure buildup.
4. To make the crust and topping, in a medium bowl, stir together the oats, flour, brown sugar, baking soda, cinnamon, and salt. Pour in the melted butter and mix to combine. The crust should be crumbly and should stick together when pressed between two fingers.
5. Evenly press two-thirds of the crust mixture into the prepared pan. Spread the apricot filling over top, then sprinkle the remaining crust mixture over the filling.
6. Bake for 30 to 35 minutes, until the top is golden brown. Allow to cool completely before slicing into squares and serving.

Storage instructions: Store in an airtight container and enjoy within 1 week.

Make it gluten-free: Use your favorite gluten-free 1-to-1 or measure-for-measure flour.

SERVES 12–16 | PREP TIME: 30 MINUTES, PLUS CHILLING TIME | COOK TIME: 45 MINUTES

Four-Berry Slab Pie

with Vanilla-Oat Streusel

Feeding a crowd? You're going to want to skip the regular pie and make a gigantic slab pie. With a thinner layer of fruit filling, it's more like a pie bar, and it's so much easier to slice and serve. A streusel topping is less hassle than arranging the perfect lattice crust, and call us crazy, but it's just the better way to top a pie. Store-bought pie crust is the easiest way to shortcut this recipe, and it will be equally delicious. When it comes to the fruit filling, our favorite combination is cherries, raspberries, blackberries, and blueberries, but you can experiment with all sorts of summer fruits or choose just one or two (keeping the same total weight) to keep it simple.

FOR THE CRUST

2½ cups all-purpose flour, plus more for dusting
2 tbsp granulated sugar
1 tsp fine sea salt
1 cup unsalted butter, cold, cut into ¼-inch (5mm) cubes
⅓–½ cup ice-cold water, as needed
1 large egg, beaten with 1 tsp water

FOR THE STREUSEL TOPPING

1 cup quick-cook oats
1 cup all-purpose flour
½ cup granulated sugar
¼ cup light brown sugar, packed
½ tsp ground cinnamon
½ cup salted butter, melted
1 tsp vanilla extract

FOR THE FILLING

18oz (500g) blueberries
1lb (450g) sweet cherries, halved
12oz (350g) raspberries
12oz (350g) blackberries
½ cup granulated sugar
⅓ cup light brown sugar, packed
⅓ cup cornstarch
1½ tbsp freshly squeezed lemon juice
1½ tsp vanilla extract
1 tsp lemon zest
½ tsp ground cinnamon
Pinch of kosher salt

TO SERVE

Vanilla ice cream

1. To make the crust, in a large bowl, whisk together the flour, sugar, and sea salt. Add the butter and using a pastry cutter or your hands, work it into the flour until the butter pieces are about the size of peas. Gradually add ⅓ cup of the ice water, stirring with a spatula, until the dough starts to form moist clumps. If the dough is still too dry, add up to ½ cup of the ice water total. Avoid overhandling the dough—there should still be visible pieces of butter.
2. Wrap the dough in plastic wrap and flatten into a rectangle. Set aside in the refrigerator for 1 hour.
3. Preheat the oven to 375°F (190°C).
4. To make the streusel topping, in a large bowl, combine the oats, flour, granulated sugar, brown sugar, and cinnamon and stir to combine. Pour in the melted butter and vanilla extract and stir until well incorporated and the mixture becomes crumbly. Set aside in the refrigerator until ready to use.
5. To make the filling, in a large bowl, combine the blueberries, cherries,

raspberries, blackberries, granulated sugar, brown sugar, cornstarch, lemon juice, vanilla extract, lemon zest, cinnamon, and salt. Stir until the fruit is well coated.

6. On a lightly floured surface, roll out the pie dough into a 16 x 20-inch (41 x 50cm) rectangle about ⅛ inch (3mm) thick. Add more flour as needed to prevent sticking. To an 18 x 13-inch (46 x 33cm) sheet pan, carefully transfer the dough and gently press into the edges of the pan. If there is excess dough overhang, trim the edges. Then, using your fingers, crimp the edges all the way around the edge of the pan.
7. Brush the edges of the crust with the beaten egg. Pour in the fruit and spread into an even layer. Top with an even layer of the streusel.
8. Bake for 45 to 55 minutes, until the crust is golden brown and the filling is bubbling. If the crust starts to brown too quickly, cover the edges loosely with strips of aluminum foil.
9. Let cool for 1 to 3 hours before serving with a scoop of vanilla ice cream.

Storage instructions: Store leftovers covered in the refrigerator for up to 3 days.

Note: When washing your fruit, make sure to drain well and pat dry with a paper towel to prevent excess moisture in the filling.

SERVES 6–8 | PREP TIME: 35 MINUTES, PLUS COOLING AND FREEZING TIME | COOK TIME: 35 MINUTES

Blackberry-Crisp Ice Cream

Beth: One summer, when Lexi was in her teens, we bought an ice cream maker and got really into making homemade ice cream. We constantly had two to three different flavors in the freezer, and since then, we've never looked back! You don't need a fancy machine to make delicious ice cream at home—there are several options well under $100 online that yield perfect results, and you'll probably save money in the long run (and have more fun in the process). Blackberry-Crisp Ice Cream takes everything you love about a warm fruit crisp and swirls it into a scoopable frozen treat. The buttery streusel stays crisp even after it's folded into the ice cream, so you get a satisfying crunch in every spoonful.

FOR THE ICE CREAM BASE

2 cups heavy cream
1 cup whole milk
⅔ cup granulated sugar
6 large egg yolks
2 tsp vanilla extract
Pinch of kosher salt

FOR THE CRISP

1 cup quick-cook oats
½ cup light brown sugar, packed
⅓ cup all-purpose flour
½ tsp ground cinnamon
Pinch of kosher salt
6 tbsp unsalted butter, cut into small cubes

FOR THE BLACKBERRY COMPOTE

2 cups fresh or frozen blackberries
⅓ cup granulated sugar
2 tbsp freshly squeezed lemon juice
1 tsp lemon zest

1. Preheat the oven to 350°F (180°C). Prepare the ice cream machine per the machine instructions.
2. To make the ice cream base, in a medium pot over medium heat, combine the heavy cream, milk, and sugar and stir well. Bring to a simmer, stirring occasionally, then reduce the heat to low.
3. In a medium bowl, whisk the egg yolks until smooth. While whisking the eggs, slowly pour in ½ cup of the hot cream mixture. Then, slowly stream the egg mixture into the pot with hot cream, whisking constantly over low heat.
4. Stir in the vanilla extract and salt and cook for 3 to 5 minutes, whisking occasionally, until the mixture starts to thicken. Once thickened, strain the mixture through a fine-mesh sieve into a medium bowl or liquid measuring cup, then set aside to cool to room temperature.
5. To make the crisp, in a large bowl, combine the oats, brown sugar, flour, cinnamon, and salt and stir to combine. Add the butter and, using a pastry cutter or your hands, work it into the other ingredients until evenly distributed and broken up into pea-size pieces. Spread the mixture onto a sheet pan and press it gently into one piece.
6. Bake for 20 to 22 minutes, until golden brown. Let cool in the sheet pan until the crisp is no longer hot to the touch, then break it into pieces.
7. To make the compote, in a medium saucepan over medium heat, combine the blackberries, sugar, lemon juice, and lemon zest. Stir well and bring to a simmer, then cook for 3 to 5 minutes, stirring occasionally, until the blackberries start to break down and slightly thicken. Transfer to a bowl to cool completely.

8. Once the ice cream base is cooled, pour into the ice cream maker and start churning. Most machines will take 20 to 30 minutes to churn. Once the ice cream is done, transfer one-third to a 32-ounce (1L) freezer-safe container, then swirl in one-third of the blackberry compote, followed by one-third of the crisp. Repeat two more times with the rest of the ingredients to ensure you get every ingredient in every bite!

9. Cover the ice cream and freeze for about 4 hours, until it's firm and scoopable. Before serving, let the ice cream thaw at room temperature for 5 to 10 minutes.

Storage instructions: Store the covered ice cream in the freezer for up to 1 month.

SERVES ABOUT 6 | PREP TIME: 5 MINUTES, PLUS FREEZING TIME

Three-Ingredient Fruit Sorbets

GF V

To this day, our three-ingredient Mango-Lime Sorbet is our most popular social media video of all time. It's racked up over a hundred million views across our platforms and for good reason! It's so easy to make, with no complicated ingredients and much less sugar than store-bought sorbet. We've customized the recipe in many ways, and these three variations are our favorites. If you want to get extra fancy, you can freeze and serve the sorbet in a hollowed-out fruit shell, but a regular bowl is perfectly fine too!

MANGO-LIME SORBET

5 cups frozen mango, slightly thawed at room temperature for 30 minutes
⅓ cup freshly squeezed lime juice
¼–⅓ cup honey or to taste

STRAWBERRY-LEMONADE SORBET

5 cups frozen strawberries, slightly thawed at room temperature for 30 minutes
¾ cup freshly squeezed lemon juice
⅓ cup honey or to taste

PEACH-RASPBERRY SORBET

3 ½ cups frozen peaches, slightly thawed at room temperature for 30 minutes
1 ½ cups frozen raspberries, slightly thawed at room temperature for 30 minutes
¼–⅓ cup honey or to taste

1. In the bowl of a food processor or a blender, combine all of the ingredients for the sorbet of your choice. Blend until completely smooth, scraping down the sides as needed. If the fruit is not slightly thawed, this may take up to 5 minutes of blending.
2. Enjoy the sorbet right away for a soft-serve consistency or transfer to a freezer-safe container, cover, and freeze for 2 to 3 hours until firm and scoopable. Let thaw at room temperature for 5 to 10 minutes before scooping and serving.

If you would like to serve the sorbet in the hollowed-out fruit as pictured here, here's how to do it for each fruit.

Mango: Cut the mangoes in half around the pit, scoop out the fruit with a spoon, then dice. Transfer the diced fruit and empty mango skins to a sheet pan lined with parchment paper and freeze for about 2 hours until solid, then continue with the recipe above, using the frozen diced mango. Scoop the sorbet into the frozen mango skins and freeze until solid.

Lemon: Slice the lemons in half lengthwise, then use a citrus reamer to remove the juice. With a spoon, scrape out the flesh and seeds. Scoop the blended sorbet into the frozen lemon halves and freeze until solid.

Peach: Cut the peaches in half and remove the pit, then carefully scoop out the fruit, leaving a small border. Transfer the diced fruit and empty peach skins to a sheet pan lined with parchment paper and freeze for about 2 hours until solid, then continue with the recipe using the frozen peaches. Scoop the sorbet into the frozen peach skins and freeze until solid.

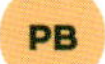

Dessert Fruit Salad

The naysayers will say, "Fruit salad isn't dessert!" And you know what? We get it. But even with a big sweet tooth, sometimes a fruit salad really is the perfect after-dinner treat, especially when you use the freshest, most seasonal ingredients. A good fruit salad isn't just chopped fruit. We always toss ours in a simple dressing made with citrus juice and zest to brighten up the flavors, a touch of honey or agave for extra sweetness, and fresh herbs for a pop of freshness. You can easily change up this recipe based on what's in season—we've provided some ideas for you to start.

- 2 tbsp freshly squeezed lime or lemon juice
- 2 tbsp agave (or honey if not plant-based)
- 1 tbsp finely chopped mint
- 2 tsp lime or lemon zest
- 10 cups fresh fruit of choice, cut into evenly sized pieces

1. In a small bowl, whisk together the lime juice, agave, mint, and lime zest until smooth.
2. To a large bowl, add the fruit and drizzle with the dressing. Toss well to coat and enjoy right away, or refrigerate for up to 48 hours.

Note: The longer this sits in the refrigerator, the soggier and softer the fruit will become.

SPRING/SUMMER FRUIT SALAD IDEAS

Fresh berries (e.g., blackberries, blueberries, strawberries, raspberries), cherries, watermelon, mango, dragon fruit, peaches or nectarines, apricots, and plums.

FALL/WINTER FRUIT SALAD IDEAS

Grapes, apples (i.e., Honeycrisp and/or Granny Smith), fresh figs, pomegranate arils, kiwi, orange or grapefruit segments, and bananas. Instead of using all lemon or lime, we like to substitute half the juice and zest with orange juice and orange zest.

MAKES 18–20 | **PREP TIME:** 10 MINUTES, PLUS CHILLING TIME

V

No-Bake S'mores Cookie Dough Bites

We love keeping a batch of cookie dough bites in the fridge or freezer for a quick dessert when you want a little sweet treat but don't want to turn the oven on. These ones are packed with s'mores components like graham cracker crumbs, mini chocolate chips, mini marshmallows, and marshmallow fluff. If we're being perfectly honest, this recipe should probably come with a warning label: These are hard to stop eating, and the batch will be gone very quickly! They're also equally delicious with or without the chocolate coating.

FOR THE COOKIE DOUGH

1¾ cup almond flour
¾ cup graham cracker crumbs, plus more for topping
½ cup mini chocolate chips
½ cup mini marshmallows, halved
½ tsp kosher salt
6 tbsp unsalted butter, melted and slightly cooled
¼ cup maple syrup
1 tsp vanilla extract
½ cup marshmallow fluff

FOR THE CHOCOLATE COATING

1 cup mini chocolate chips
1 tbsp coconut oil

1. Line a sheet pan with parchment paper.
2. To make the cookie dough, in a large bowl, stir together the almond flour, graham cracker crumbs, mini chocolate chips, mini marshmallows, and salt. Pour in the melted butter, maple syrup, and vanilla extract and stir until combined. Add the marshmallow fluff and stir for a few minutes until fully incorporated.
3. Using a tablespoon, portion the dough into 18 to 20 pieces. With your hands, roll each portion into a ball. Place the balls on the prepared sheet pan.
4. To make the chocolate coating, in a small microwave-safe bowl, combine the chocolate chips and coconut oil. Microwave in 30-second intervals, stirring well in between, until the chocolate is fully melted.
5. Using two forks, dip each cookie dough ball into the melted chocolate. Let the excess chocolate drip off before returning it to the parchment paper.
6. Place the bites in the refrigerator for about 20 minutes, until the chocolate sets and enjoy.

Storage instructions: Transfer to an airtight container and store in the refrigerator for 2 weeks, or in the freezer for 3 months.

Make it gluten-free: Use gluten-free graham crackers instead of traditional ones.

MAKES 18 | PREP TIME: 35 MINUTES, PLUS COOLING TIME COOK TIME: 25 MINUTES

Neapolitan Cupcakes
with Strawberry Buttercream

Perfect for parties, bake sales, or whenever you're feeling a little nostalgic, these cupcakes capture the charm of a classic childhood treat in cupcake form. A three-layer cupcake might look complicated, but you only need to mix one batter. Once the base vanilla layer is made, simply divide the batter in three and add cocoa and strawberry powder to each respective flavor. Freeze-dried strawberries really pack a flavor punch, especially in the strawberry buttercream. (And yes, that vibrant pink hue is all natural!)

FOR THE CUPCAKES

2½ cups plus 1½ tbsp cake flour, divided
1 tbsp baking powder
¾ tsp fine sea salt
2 cups granulated sugar
1 cup vegetable oil
1 tbsp vanilla extract
2 large eggs
1 cup whole milk
1 tbsp freshly squeezed lemon juice
½oz (14g) strawberry powder, sifted (see note)
2 tbsp Dutch-process cocoa powder, sifted

FOR THE STRAWBERRY-BUTTERCREAM FROSTING

1 cup salted butter, softened
6 tbsp heavy cream
3–3½ cups powdered sugar, sifted
1oz (28g) freeze-dried strawberry powder, sifted
1 tsp vanilla extract
Pinch of kosher salt
Sprinkles, to serve (optional)

1. Preheat the oven to 350°F (180°C). Line two muffin tins with 18 paper liners.
2. To make the cupcakes, in a medium bowl, whisk together 2½ cups of the cake flour and the baking powder and salt.
3. In a separate large bowl, combine the granulated sugar, vegetable oil, and vanilla extract. Using a hand mixer on medium speed, mix for about 30 seconds, until smooth and evenly hydrated, then add in the eggs and beat on medium-high for 1 minute, until no streaks remain. Pour in the milk and lemon juice and mix on low speed until combined. Working in three batches, add the dry ingredients, mixing between each addition, until a smooth batter forms.
4. Divide the batter evenly over three medium or large bowls. To one bowl, add the sifted strawberry powder, to another the sifted cocoa powder, and to the third bowl the remaining 1½ tablespoons cake flour. Whisk each bowl until just combined, but do not overmix.
5. To each muffin liner, add 1 tablespoon of the chocolate batter, then 1 tablespoon of the strawberry batter, and 1 tablespoon of the vanilla batter. Be careful not to overfill the muffin tins.
6. Bake for 21 to 23 minutes, until the tops are golden brown and a toothpick inserted into the center of a cupcake comes out mostly clean. Let cool in the pan for 5 minutes, then transfer to a wire cooling rack to cool completely before frosting.
7. To make the frosting, in a large bowl, add the butter and heavy cream and using a hand mixer, whisk on medium speed for 1 to 2 minutes, until fluffy. Add 3 cups of the powdered sugar and the freeze-dried strawberry powder, vanilla, and salt and beat on medium speed for 2 to 3 minutes, until well-combined, light, and fluffy. If too wet and runny, whisk in the remaining powdered sugar.
8. Frost the cooled cupcakes and top with sprinkles (if using) before serving.

Note: To turn freeze-dried strawberries into a powder, pulse them in a food processor. Sift through a fine-mesh sieve to remove the seeds.

MAKES ONE 8 X 8-INCH (20 X 20CM) PAN | PREP TIME: 20 MINUTES COOK TIME: 1 HOUR

Dad's Scottish Shortbread

V

Lexi: There's only one dessert my dad can successfully make, and it's this shortbread. (Sorry, Dad!) Thanks to his Scottish heritage, we've been enjoying these cookies for as long as I can remember, and they're just as buttery, rich, and melt-in-your-mouth delicious as you can imagine. The basic version is fantastic, but over the years, we've also experimented with some seasonal variations, which are all included here.

⅔ cup granulated sugar
1 tsp vanilla extract
2 cups all-purpose flour
¼ cup cornstarch
½ tsp kosher salt
1 cup unsalted butter, softened and cut into small pieces

1. Preheat the oven to 300°F (180°C). Line an 8 x 8-inch (20 x 20 cm) pan with parchment paper, allowing the edges to overhang for easy removal after baking.
2. In a small bowl, combine the granulated sugar and vanilla extract. Using your hands, massage the vanilla into the sugar.
3. In a large bowl, stir together the flour, cornstarch, salt, and vanilla-infused sugar. Add the softened butter pieces to the bowl. Using your hands, mix and knead the dough for 3 to 5 minutes, until a solid ball forms.
4. Press the dough evenly into the prepared pan. With a fork, dock the surface of the dough in evenly spaced intervals. Bake for 55 to 60 minutes, until the edges are light golden brown.
5. While still hot, carefully remove the shortbread from the pan, place atop a cutting board, and use a sharp knife to slice the shortbread into squares of your preferred size.

ORANGE CHOCOLATE

To the sugar and vanilla extract, add 1½ tablespoons of orange zest and massage for 30 seconds. Into the flour mixture, stir ½ cup of mini semisweet chocolate chips, then proceed with the base recipe.

LEMON LAVENDER

To the sugar and vanilla extract, add 2 tablespoons of lemon zest and 1½ teaspoons of culinary-grade lavender. Massage for about 30 seconds before incorporating into the dough as directed in the base recipe.

CHERRY LIME

Finely chop ½ cup of unsweetened dried cherries and stir into the flour mixture. In place of the vanilla, combine the sugar with 1½ tablespoons of lime zest, ½ teaspoon of vanilla extract, and ½ teaspoon of almond extract and massage for 30 seconds before adding to the dough. (If avoiding almond extract, use additional vanilla extract instead.)

SERVES 10 | **PREP TIME:** 15 MINUTES, PLUS FREEZING TIME **COOK TIME:** 10 MINUTES

Buckeye Bars

If you're not from the Midwest, you may not be familiar with buckeyes, the sweet treat of choice for many of our family gatherings. Essentially, they're super-sweet peanut butter balls covered in chocolate and look like the nuts from a buckeye tree, and they've made an appearance at every single family Christmas we've ever had. In true Midwestern form, we made them even more decadent by turning them into bars with a peanut and graham cracker crust, a creamy peanut butter filling, and a layer of chocolate ganache. Need we say more?

FOR THE CRUST

- 1 cup graham cracker crumbs
- ½ cup roasted, lightly salted peanuts
- 6 tbsp salted butter, melted
- 3 tbsp granulated sugar
- 1 tsp vanilla extract

FOR THE FILLING

- 2 cups powdered sugar
- 1 cup oat flour
- ½ tsp ground cinnamon
- ¼ tsp kosher salt
- 1½ cups creamy natural peanut butter
- ½ cup salted butter, softened
- 2 tsp vanilla extract

FOR THE TOPPING

- ½ cup half-and-half
- 12oz (345g) mini semisweet chocolate chips
- Flaky sea salt, to garnish

1. Line a 9 x 9-inch (23 x 23cm) baking pan with parchment paper.
2. To make the crust, in a food processor, pulse together the graham crackers and peanuts until a fine, crumb-like mixture forms. Add the melted butter, sugar, and vanilla extract and pulse again until well incorporated.
3. Press the crust mixture evenly into the bottom of the prepared pan and place in the freezer for 30 minutes while making the filling.
4. To make the filling, in a medium bowl, sift the powdered sugar, oat flour, cinnamon, and salt. Mix to combine. To a separate large bowl, add the peanut butter, butter, and vanilla extract. Using an electric mixer on medium speed, beat for about 5 minutes, until smooth. Working in two batches, add the sifted dry ingredients, mixing well between each addition, until a smooth batter forms.
5. Remove the crust from the freezer. Evenly spread the peanut-butter filling over the crust. Refrigerate uncovered for at least 30 minutes, ideally an hour, until the peanut butter is firm.
6. To make the topping, about 10 minutes before removing the bars from the fridge, in a small saucepan over medium heat, add the half-and-half and heat until lightly simmering. To a medium heat-safe bowl, add the chocolate chips, then immediately pour the hot half-and-half over top. Let sit for 2 minutes, then whisk until smooth.
7. Evenly spread the chocolate ganache over the peanut butter filling. Sprinkle with flaky sea salt and refrigerate for at least 3 hours to set before slicing.

Storage instructions: Store in an airtight container in the refrigerator for up to 1 week.

SERVES 10–12 | **PREP TIME: 20 MINUTES, PLUS COOLING TIME** **COOK TIME: 1 HOUR**

Pomegranate-Cranberry Caramels

Lexi: Growing up, my grandpa (Beth's dad) used to make caramels every Christmas, and it was always the treat I most looked forward to! We created this recipe in his memory, with a bit of a sophisticated twist that makes them somehow even more delicious. Pomegranate and cranberry juice are boiled down into a syrup that's used for the base of these caramels. The tartness really comes through, which makes these much less cloyingly sweet than most caramels. These are an excellent DIY gift for friends, family, hosts and hostesses, and more at the holidays!

- 2 cups no-sugar-added pomegranate juice
- 2 cups no-sugar-added cranberry juice
- Peel from ½ an orange, pith removed
- Nonstick spray
- 1 cup unsalted butter, cut into cubes
- ¾ cup granulated sugar
- ¾ cup light brown sugar, packed
- ⅓ cup heavy cream
- 2 tsp vanilla extract
- 1 tsp kosher salt

1. In a heavy-bottomed saucepan over medium heat, combine the pomegranate juice, cranberry juice, and orange peel. Bring to a light boil, then reduce the heat to medium-low and let simmer, whisking infrequently. The mixture will bubble significantly when whisked. Reduce the mixture until about a ½ cup of syrup remains. You'll know it's done when a spatula dragged across the bottom of the pan leaves a visible path before the syrup slowly covers the area again. The syrup should be thick and coat the back of a spoon. Timing will depend on a lot of factors, but for us, it takes about an hour, give or take 10 minutes.
2. While the syrup is reducing, lightly spray an 8 x 8-inch (20 x 20cm) pan with nonstick spray and line it with parchment paper, ensuring the paper covers the sides for easy removal.
3. Using tongs, remove the orange peel from the reduced syrup and with the heat remaining on medium-low, add the butter, both sugars, and the heavy cream. Cook and stir until the butter is melted and the sugar has dissolved. Attach a candy thermometer to the side of the pan, increase the heat to medium, and bring to a boil.
4. For softer caramels, heat to between 245°F and 250°F (118°C and 121°C). For firmer caramels *(recommended)*, heat to between 255°F and 260°F (124°F and 127°C). Once the mixture reaches the desired temperature, remove from the heat and immediately whisk in the vanilla extract and salt.
5. Carefully pour the caramel into the prepared pan. Place the pan in the refrigerator for about 1½ hours to cool and fully set.
6. Once set, transfer the caramel slab to a cutting board, keeping the parchment underneath to prevent sticking. Lightly grease a knife with nonstick spray and cut the caramels into ½-inch x 1½-inch (1cm x 3.5cm) rectangles. Wrap the individual pieces in wax paper to prevent sticking and enjoy.

Storage instructions: Store in an airtight container at room temp. for up to 1 month. If too soft, placing in the freezer for 10 minutes will make them chewier.

AMARO
BONAL
GENTIANE-QUINA
BONAL
ST-GERMAIN
CHARTREUSE
Amaro
1885
ABSOLUT
ELYX
SINGLE ESTATE
COPPER CRAFTED
VODKA
1800
TEQUILA
Blanco
STEWART
DRUNKEN BOTANIST
CURE
BODENHEIMER AND TIMBERLAKE

Extras

MAKES A 16OZ (500ML) JAR | PREP TIME: 10 MINUTES COOK TIME: 5 MINUTES

Quick Pickles

Homemade quick-pickled vegetables are easier to make than you think—and so versatile! Unlike regular pickles, these do not require water bath canning. That also means they won't last as long, so you'll have to keep them stored in the refrigerator and consume within a few weeks, but it's such a quick and easy way to add crunchy, briny flavor to bowls, sandwiches, burgers, tacos, salads, and more—so eating it all before it goes bad shouldn't be an issue.

FOR THE VEGETABLES (CHOOSE ONE)

1 large red onion, thinly sliced
2 cups thinly sliced red cabbage
2 cups thinly sliced radishes
2 cups thinly sliced jalapeños
2 cups thinly sliced cucumbers (ideally pickling cucumbers)

FOR SEASONING (CHOOSE AS MANY AS DESIRED)

¼ cup chopped dill
1 tbsp whole peppercorns
2–3 garlic cloves, lightly crushed
2–3 sprigs thyme or rosemary
1½ tsp pickling spices

FOR A BASIC BRINE

1 cup distilled white vinegar
2 tsp kosher salt
1 tsp granulated sugar

1. In a clean 16-ounce (500ml) glass jar, pack your desired vegetable and optional seasonings.
2. To make the brine, in a small saucepan over medium-high heat, combine 1 cup of water and the vinegar, salt, and sugar. Bring to a simmer, stirring occasionally, until the sugar and salt are dissolved.
3. Remove from the heat and let cool for 5 minutes. Pour the brine directly into the glass jar, making sure to cover the produce completely. Let the jars cool to room temperature, then cover and refrigerate.

Storage instructions: Most quick-pickled vegetables will last for about 1 month in the refrigerator, but onions and shallots will only last for 2 weeks. If you notice any cloudiness, mold, or an "off" smell, discard immediately.

MAKES 1 CUP | PREP TIME: 10 MINUTES

Easy Homemade Pesto

Although we often use good-quality store-bought pesto in a pinch (our favorite brand is Gotham Greens!), this is our go-to recipe when we have plenty of basil growing in our garden in the summer. Use it on sandwiches, pizza or flatbread, pasta, drizzled on salads or soups, and so much more.

2 cups basil, lightly packed
¼ cup pine nuts
1 garlic clove
1 tbsp freshly squeezed lemon juice
1 tsp lemon zest
½ cup olive oil, plus more as needed
⅓ cup grated Parmesan
Kosher salt, to taste
Ground black pepper, to taste

1. In a food processor, combine the basil, pine nuts, garlic, lemon juice, and lemon zest. Pulse until everything is finely chopped. With the machine running, slowly drizzle in the olive oil until the mixture is smooth.
2. Add the Parmesan and season with salt and pepper to taste. Pulse until just combined. Taste and adjust seasoning as desired. For a looser pesto, add an extra 1 to 2 tablespoons of olive oil.

Storage instructions: Store in the fridge in an airtight container for up to 2 weeks.

Make it plant-based: Substitute the Parmesan with your favorite plant-based alternative or use nutritional yeast for a similar cheesy flavor.

SERVES 4–6 | PREP TIME: 5 MINUTES COOK TIME: 20 MINUTES

Cilantro-Lime Rice

We make this all the time for homemade burrito bowls, and it's also the perfect base for our Fish Taco Bowls (page 128). It's an easy way to upgrade basic white rice for a more flavorful weeknight dinner!

1½ cups long-grain white rice, rinsed
3 tbsp chopped cilantro
2 tbsp freshly squeezed lime juice
1½ tbsp avocado or olive oil
1½ tsp kosher salt

1. To a medium saucepan over high heat, add the rinsed rice and 3 cups of water and bring to a boil. Then reduce the heat to low and cover with a lid. Let cook for 15 to 20 minutes, until the water is completely absorbed.
2. When the rice is done, fluff with a fork and stir in the cilantro, lime juice, oil, and salt until well incorporated. Serve hot.

MAKES ABOUT ¼ CUP | PREP TIME: 5 MINUTES

 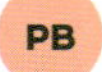

Basil Oil

We love to add a swirl of this herbaceous oil to summery soups, salads (especially a caprese), pasta, grilled chicken or shrimp, and more. Try the spicy version with fresh minced jalapeño for a little kick.

½ cup roughly chopped basil
¼ cup olive oil
1 tbsp minced jalapeño (optional)
1½ tsp freshly squeezed lemon juice
¼ tsp kosher salt
¼ tsp ground black pepper

1. In a small food processor or blender, combine the basil, oil, jalapeño (if using), lemon juice, salt, and pepper. Blend for 15 to 30 seconds, until the basil leaves have broken down. If you don't have a small enough blender, you can finely chop all the ingredients instead and stir them together in a bowl. If following that method, for maximum flavor, let the oil sit for 30 minutes at room temperature before using.

MAKES 1 CUP | PREP TIME: 5 MINUTES COOK TIME: 5 MINUTES

Homemade Hot Honey

Hot honey is having a serious moment, and for good reason. It's one of our all-time favorite condiments for drizzling on pizzas, salads, and crostini, and of course on our Hot Honey Panko Chicken Cutlets (page 145). This version is pretty spicy, so if you prefer milder heat, cut the red pepper flakes and jalapeño quantities in half.

1 cup honey
1 small jalapeño, thinly sliced
1 tsp red pepper flakes

1. In a small saucepan over medium heat, combine the honey, jalapeño, and red pepper flakes. Bring to a gentle simmer and cook for about 5 minutes, stirring occasionally, until the honey is loose, then remove from the heat and let steep for 5 to 10 minutes. Strain through a fine-mesh sieve and let cool completely before transferring to an airtight container. Discard the solids after straining.

Storage instructions: Store at room temperature for up to a year.

MAKES 3 CUPS | PREP TIME: 10 MINUTES COOK TIME: 1 HOUR

Classic Candied Nuts

The classic version of these candied nuts is like what you'd get at a fair. They have a super crunchy, sugary coating that makes them hard to put down, so they're great for enjoying by the handful or chopping up and garnishing a salad.

Cooking spray or neutral oil
1 large egg white
2 tsp vanilla extract
1½ cups unsalted pecans
1½ cups unsalted almonds
½ cup granulated sugar
¼ cup light brown sugar, packed
1 tsp kosher salt
1 tsp ground cinnamon
¼ tsp ground nutmeg
⅛ tsp ground cloves
Pinch of cayenne pepper (optional)

1. Position a rack in the middle of the oven and preheat to 250°F (120°C). Lightly grease a nonstick sheet pan with the cooking spray or neutral oil.
2. In a large bowl, whisk together the egg white, 1 tablespoon of water, and the vanilla extract until frothy. Add in the pecans and almonds and stir until well coated.
3. In a separate small bowl, whisk together the granulated sugar, brown sugar, salt, cinnamon, nutmeg, cloves, and cayenne pepper (if using). Pour the sugar mixture over the nuts and stir well until evenly coated.
4. Spread the nuts in an even layer on the prepared sheet pan. Bake on the middle rack for 55 to 60 minutes, stirring every 15 minutes, until the nuts no longer look wet and the sugar has caramelized. Remove from the oven, stir, and let cool completely before enjoying.

Storage instructions: Store in an airtight container at room temperature for up to 2 weeks.

MAKES ½ CUP | PREP TIME: 5 MINUTES COOK TIME: 5 MINUTES

Quick Candied Nuts

The quick version doesn't get the same super-crunchy coating, but they're still delicious and much faster to make. Plus, they're egg-free. We like to use these in our Michigan Cherry Salad (page 103).

1 tbsp granulated sugar
1 tbsp light brown sugar, packed
¼ tsp vanilla extract
⅛ tsp ground cinnamon
Pinch of kosher salt
½ cup unsalted pecans or walnuts

1. Line a small sheet pan with parchment paper.
2. Place a medium skillet over medium heat and add 1 tablespoon of water, the granulated sugar, brown sugar, vanilla extract, cinnamon, and salt. Cook for about 1 minute, stirring often, until the mixture is bubbling and the sugar has completely dissolved.
3. Stir in the nuts and cook for about 3 minutes, stirring continuously, until most of the liquid has evaporated and the nuts start to stick together.
4. Transfer the nuts to the prepared sheet pan and spread into an even layer. Let cool completely before using.

STRAWBERRY
LAVENDER
ORANGE

MAKES 1½ CUPS | PREP TIME: 5 MINUTES COOK TIME: 5 MINUTES, PLUS INFUSING TIME

PB

Infused Simple Syrups

Homemade simple syrups are the quickest and easiest way to upgrade your cocktails, mocktails, and more. You can infuse them with just about any fruit, herb, vegetable, or spice—we've listed a few of our favorites below!

FOR THE SIMPLE SYRUP

1 cup granulated sugar

TO INFUSE (CHOOSE ONE)

2 small jalapeños, sliced

4 tsp dried culinary-grade lavender

1 piece of fresh ginger, about 2 inches (5cm) thick, sliced thinly

1 handful of fresh herbs of choice (basil, thyme, mint, rosemary, etc.)

4 cinnamon sticks

1½ cups fresh berries (strawberries, blueberries, blackberries, raspberries, etc.)

1 cup freshly squeezed orange juice (in place of the water) and 1 tablespoon orange zest

A small handful of whole spices (star anise, cardamom, cloves, cinnamon, etc.)

2 mini cucumbers, sliced into rounds

1. To a small pot over medium-low heat, add 1 cup of water, the sugar, and your infusion ingredient(s) of choice. Stir and cook for about 5 minutes, until the sugar is fully dissolved and the mixture is steaming. Remove from the heat and let sit to infuse for 15 to 45 minutes. Ingredients like herbs and spices need less time, but you can leave ingredients like fresh produce to infuse for longer.
2. Strain the syrup through a fine-mesh sieve. If using fresh fruit, make sure to press as much liquid through as possible, then discard the strained solids.

Storage instructions: Store the cooled syrup in an airtight container in the refrigerator for up to 1 month.

Our Favorite Infused Alcohols

To make any cocktail taste extra special, infuse your liquor with fresh fruits, vegetables, and herbs and spices. An infused spirit also makes for a great DIY gift for friends, family, and hosts. The options are endless, but below are a few of our favorite combinations. Once you strain out the fresh ingredients, these will keep for up to a year at room temperature or in the refrigerator.

STRAWBERRY-INFUSED VODKA

MAKES A 32OZ (1L) JAR
PREP TIME: 10 MINUTES
TOTAL TIME: 1–4 WEEKS

3 cups quartered strawberries
1 vanilla bean, split in half lengthwise (optional)
750ml vodka

1. Fill a clean 32-ounce (1L) jar with the strawberries and vanilla bean (if using), then pour the vodka over top, making sure the strawberries are fully submerged.
2. Cover with a lid, then let sit in a cool, dark place at room temperature for 1 to 4 weeks. The longer it infuses, the stronger the flavor will be. Strain through a fine-mesh sieve, pressing as much liquid from the strawberries through as possible, then discard the strawberries.

JALAPEÑO-INFUSED TEQUILA

MAKES A 32OZ (1L) JAR
PREP TIME: 10 MINUTES
TOTAL TIME: 12–24 HOURS

3 small jalapeños, thinly sliced
750ml tequila

1. Fill a clean 32-ounce (1L) jar with the jalapeño slices, then pour the tequila over top.
2. Cover with a lid, then let sit in a cool, dark place at room temperature for 12 to 24 hours. The longer it infuses, the spicier the tequila will be. Strain through a fine-mesh sieve and discard the jalapeños. This is an excellent way to make a spicy margarita!

APPLE PIE-INFUSED BOURBON

MAKES A 32OZ (1L) JAR
PREP TIME: 10 MINUTES
TOTAL TIME: 3–14 DAYS

- 3 medium apples, sliced or diced (we use a mix of Honeycrisp and Granny Smith)
- ¾ cup maple syrup
- 3 cinnamon sticks
- 2–3 cardamom pods
- ¼ tsp ground nutmeg
- 3 whole cloves
- 750ml bourbon or whiskey

1. Fill a clean 32-ounce (1L) jar with the apples, maple syrup, cinnamon sticks, cardamom pods, nutmeg, and cloves, then pour the bourbon over top, making sure the apples are fully submerged.
2. Cover with a lid, then let sit in a cool, dark place at room temperature for 3 to 14 days. The longer it infuses, the stronger the flavor will be. Strain through a fine-mesh sieve, pressing as much liquid from the apples through as possible, then discard the apples.

SPICED PINEAPPLE-INFUSED RUM

MAKES A 32OZ (1L) JAR
PREP TIME: 10 MINUTES
COOK TIME: 5 MINUTES
TOTAL TIME: 3–14 DAYS

- 1 star anise
- 4 whole allspice berries
- 5 whole cloves
- 8 whole peppercorns
- 2–3 cardamom pods
- 2 cinnamon sticks, broken in half
- 3 cups diced pineapple
- 1 vanilla bean pod, sliced lengthwise (optional)
- 3 orange peels, about 1 inch (2.5cm) thick
- 1 piece of ginger, about 1 inch (2.5cm) thick
- ¼ tsp grated nutmeg
- 750ml white rum

1. In a small skillet over medium-low heat, toast the star anise, allspice berries, cloves, peppercorns, cardamom pods, and cinnamon sticks for about 5 minutes, stirring occasionally, until fragrant.
2. To a clean 32-ounce (1L) jar, add the toasted spices, pineapple, vanilla bean (if using), orange peels, ginger, and nutmeg, then pour the rum over top, making sure the pineapples are fully submerged.
3. Cover with a lid, then let sit in a cool, dark place at room temperature for 3 to 14 days. The longer it infuses, the stronger the flavor will be. Strain through a fine-mesh sieve, pressing as much liquid from the pineapple through as possible, then discard the pineapple.

Acknowledgments

To Mom (Beth), from Lexi: Building this business together has been one of the most special experiences of my life. I will forever be grateful for the opportunity to work together, which never would have been possible without your unwavering support, boundless creativity, and endless patience and love. You are the best person I know—thank you for everything.

To Lexi, from Mom (Beth): Every day, I feel so blessed to have had the opportunity to create this business together! Going back to when I coached you in high school, we have always made a great team. Your passion, dedication, creativity, and enthusiasm have made this experience an incredible journey. I love you so very much! My hope is that these recipes will serve as a reminder of our family's traditions and the memories we have shared together around the table.

To Brent, from Lexi: My wonderful partner, best friend, biggest supporter, and the man that keeps Crowded Kitchen running behind the scenes. I couldn't do any of this without you, and I love you so much.

To Todd, from Beth: My husband, self-appointed CDO (Chief Dishwashing Officer), last-minute grocery shopper, and our star taste-tester, I love you very much! I could have never done this without your constant support, love, and encouragement.

To our family, and to our friends who feel like family: It's your love and support that got us here in the first place. So many of the recipes in this book were inspired by the special people in our lives and the wonderful memories we've made together. We hope you know how much you mean to us.

To Sarah Benson and Alana Lieberman: This book might not have had any photos without the two of you. Thank you for making this such a seamless and joyful experience. We quite literally could not have done this without you. Your friendship and support mean the world to us!

To our wonderful publishing team: Alexander Rigby, Joanna Price, Emily Stephenson, Tiffany Taing, and Robert Naugle. Alex, thank you for believing in us and for bringing this cookbook to life. We so appreciate your patience and guidance. Joanna, thank you for bringing our vision to fruition—it turned out to be just as colorful and fun as we were hoping. We will forever be so grateful for this opportunity.

To Nathaniel Smith: Thank you for spending two crazy days with us to capture some of our favorite moments from this book.

To our management, Will Martin: You've been with us every step of the way on this project and we never would have stayed on track without you. Thank you for your patience and dedication. (And for answering countless text messages and voice notes!)

And lastly, to the millions of wonderful people who have supported our business along the way: A massive thank you for your words of encouragement, your support of our recipes, and for getting us to this point! This book is for you.

Index

C

D

E

F

G

M

N

O

Q

R

S

About the Authors

Beth Sinclair and Lexi Harrison are the mother-daughter team behind Crowded Kitchen, a popular food blog that shares a wide range of approachable food and drink recipes. With a focus on seasonal ingredients and ideas for feeding a family with multiple dietary preferences, Crowded Kitchen aims to solve the needs of the modern home chef.